CONTENTS

Above. A painted panel in the Royal Palace displays the date of birth of James VI, the only monarch known to have been born at Edinburgh Castle, on 19 June 1566.

HIGHLIGHTS

A ROYAL PALACE
58–65 *Below*

Edinburgh's royal connections date back 1,000 years, and for a time in the 1400s and 1500s it was among Scotland's chief royal residences.

THE GREAT HALL
42 *Right*

Built around 1510 for James IV, to house grand banquets and other state events, the Great Hall was later used for military purposes, and afterwards given a Victorian makeover, but it retains its superb late-medieval ceiling.

A MILITARY STRONGHOLD
72–77

Always well defended, the castle has long been an important military base, right up to the present day.

THE ONE O'CLOCK GUN
14

You can set your watch by the time signal, fired from Mills Mount Battery daily (except Sundays, Christmas Day and Good Friday) at precisely 1300 hours.

ST MARGARET'S CHAPEL
22 *Left*

The oldest building in Edinburgh, this modest chapel was built around 1130 by King David I, as a tribute to his devout mother.

THE NATIONAL SHRINE
44 *Right*

Standing on Crown Square at the centre of the castle, the Scottish National War Memorial pays solemn tribute to those who lost their lives in the First World War and later conflicts.

THE STONE OF DESTINY
41 *Below*

Scotland's ancient kingmaking stone was removed by the invading English king Edward I in 1296, but has been kept at the castle since its return in 1996.

THE HONOURS OF SCOTLAND
38 *Below*

Britain's oldest crown jewels, the Crown, Sword and Sceptre are displayed in a specially fortified room built for them in the 1600s.

PANORAMIC VIEWS
10–13

Edinburgh Castle sits at the heart of a UNESCO World Heritage Site and affords superb views across the city, to Fife and beyond in the north and across the Pentland Hills to the south.

ARTILLERY DEFENCES
8, 24, 30–31

The huge late-medieval siege cannon Mons Meg takes pride of place among numerous artillery pieces that bristle from the castle's many batteries.

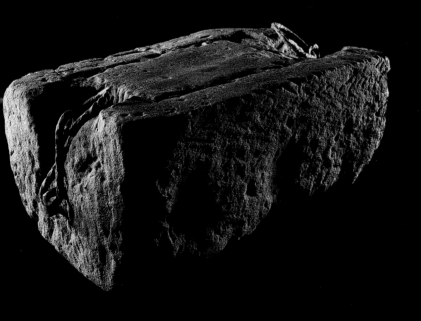

EXPLORE THE CASTLE

The buildings and fortifications now standing on the Castle Rock developed over hundreds of years – and in most cases, they replaced even older structures. The needs of this royal stronghold have changed constantly over the centuries, and it has been remodelled accordingly.

At times, parts of it were destroyed beyond repair. At other times, new threats and new military technologies demanded new fortifications. But this has always been a relatively secure stronghold, a place of military strength where royalty could reside safely and priceless national treasures could be stored. It has never been easy to capture.

This section describes the buildings, treasures and other key features of the castle, explaining how each development was prompted by its changing role.

Guided tours are also provided free of charge by well-informed castle guides; and audio guides are available for hire. The numbers given next to certain headings refer to equivalent points on the audio guide – look for black shields with white numbers. Note that numbers 22 and 23 have been reversed due to a change in routing.

Right. A view of the castle from Princes Street.

1 THE CASTLE GATES

The eastern side of the castle has always been the main approach to the mighty Castle Rock. Compared with the other three sides, which are steep, dangerous crags, this approach was relatively easy to climb. But this also made it vulnerable. Consequently, it has seen remarkable change over the centuries.

The Portcullis Gate

This fortified archway was built as the principal gateway into the castle in the 1570s. This was part of a major programme of repairs, after a three-year siege known as the Lang Siege.

This gateway originally had four barriers – an iron portcullis and three pairs of wooden doors. You can still see the iron crooks on which the heavy doors were hung.

 The Portcullis Gate from outside the shop looks great in the morning. Close-up detailed shots of the studs on the wooden doors work really well, and try the spikes on the portcullis.

2 THE LANG STAIRS

Next to the Portcullis Gate is a steep flight of 70 steps, aptly named the Lang Stairs. This was the main route to the summit in medieval times. The stairs once passed beneath the tall Constable's Tower, which was destroyed during the Lang Siege. The curved wall on the right of the stairs may have formed part of that tower.

A plaque high up on the wall commemorates the successful assault on the castle by Sir Thomas Randolph, Earl of Moray, in 1314, during the Wars of Independence with England. The date of 1313 given on the plaque is inaccurate.

Rather than struggling up the Lang Stairs, take the curved cobbled road ahead, a more leisurely route to the summit. This approach was formed in the 1600s to ease the movement of heavy guns in and out of the castle. The central strip of small granite pieces provided better grip for the horses' hooves.

1 The Portcullis Gate, once defended by three pairs of gates as well as the portcullis.

2 The Lang Stairs, once the main route to the heart of the castle.

3 One of the iron crooks in the Portcullis Gate from which an inner door once hung.

4 One of a pair of carved stone lions on the outside of the Portcullis Gate. It represented the Scottish king and was probably painted in bright colours.

5 Stone plaque commemorating the capture of the castle by Thomas Randolph, Earl of Moray, in 1314 (see page 60). The date shown on the plaque is incorrect.

TO COMMEMORATE
THOMAS RANDOLPH
EARL OF MORAY
A DISTINGUISHED SOLD
IER AND DIPLOMATIST
WHO RECOVERED THIS
CASTLE IN 1313 AFTER
IT HAD BEEN FOR 20
YEARS IN THE HAND
OF THE ENGLISH

1 The Argyle Battery, facing north, was built during the era of the Jacobite Risings.

2 The Cartshed, completed just after the last Jacobite Rising of 1745–6.

1

3 THE ARGYLE BATTERY

This six-gun artillery battery was built in the 1730s. It was named after the 2nd Duke of Argyll, commander of an army that halted the advance of a much larger Jacobite force at Sheriffmuir in 1715.

The battery was designed by Captain John Romer, a military engineer, better known for designing mighty Fort Augustus, and built by William Adam, better known for designing great country houses.

The guns are not the original armaments. They are muzzle-loading 18-pounders, made around 1810, and on loan from the Royal Armouries. The royal cipher GR3 (for King George III) appears on the top of each barrel.

The Cartshed

The building that now houses the Redcoat Café was built in the 1600s as a storekeeper's house. It was extended to the front in 1746 to form a cartshed.

This was one of many adaptations to military premises made after the Battle of Culloden (1746), which ended the fifth and final Jacobite Rising. By this date the castle was crammed with government troops. This shed held 50 carts that brought provisions up from the town to the garrison. Should the soldiers be called out, the supply carts would feed them on the move.

Unearthed

Archaeologists excavating in front of the Cartshed were amazed to discover part of the first settlement in this shoulder of the Castle Rock. It was buried six metres below the present surface, indicating that this area has been artificially levelled up, a process that began as early as 900 BC.

The Bronze Age occupants of this settlement probably created the first defences, enclosing a very large area. Their most important people always lived on the upper terraces, where Crown Square is today.

A thousand years later, in the 1st and 2nd centuries AD, the rock had been transformed into a massive Iron Age hill fort, probably a capital of the native Votadini tribe. The rock was probably quite densely covered with timber houses, yards and outbuildings. Excavations at the front of the castle have shown that the entrance to the fort was protected by a pair of massive ditches cut through the rock. Deep beneath the front of the Cartshed, the archaeologists found substantial remains of large round-houses with heather-strewn stone floors, hearths and drains.

These Iron Age residents lived well on meat from domesticated herds – chiefly cattle – with access to food from an extensive hinterland. Wider trade was also taking place with the Romanised communities south of Hadrian's Wall, represented by fine metal brooches and pottery. The Votadini may have made peace with the Roman military and trade goods may have been gained as a result.

Above. A 2,000-year-old bronze brooch, one of two found at the castle, probably the result of trade with the Romans.

VIEWS FROM THE CASTLE

Inchcolm island

Inverleith Park

Charlotte Square

Castle Street

Visitors to the castle can enjoy views of the city and well beyond. The Argyle Battery (this page) provides views to the north, north-east and north-west.

Over the page, some key landmarks are identified.

Panoramic views of the New Town work very well in most weather conditions other than fog! Best early in the morning for shadows and depth.

Fife

Firth of Forth

Royal Botanic Garden

George Street

Frederick Street

Princes Street

Princes Street Gardens

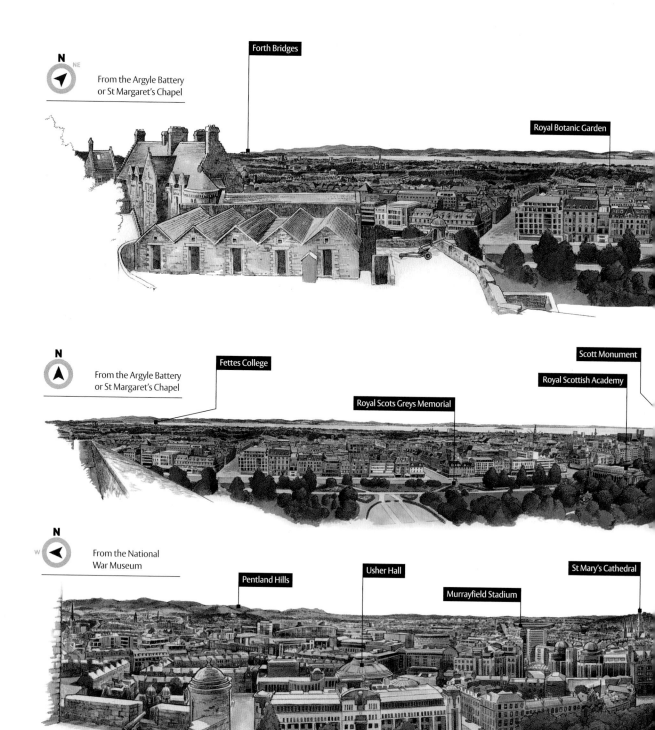

N NE
From the Argyle Battery
or St Margaret's Chapel

Forth Bridges

Royal Botanic Garden

N
From the Argyle Battery
or St Margaret's Chapel

Fettes College

Royal Scots Greys Memorial

Scott Monument

Royal Scottish Academy

N W
From the National
War Museum

Pentland Hills

Usher Hall

Murrayfield Stadium

St Mary's Cathedral

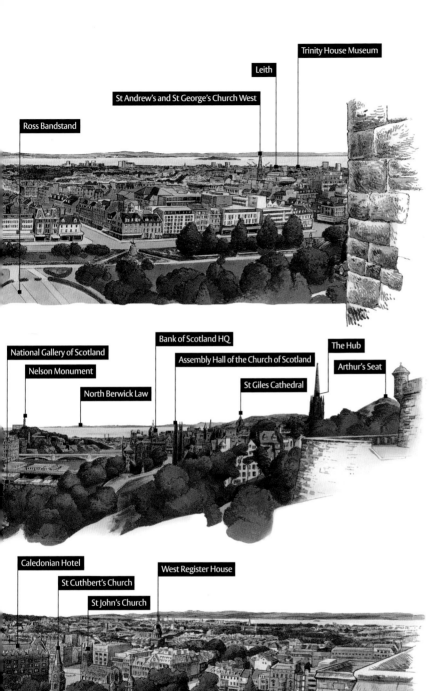

Ross Bandstand

St Andrew's and St George's Church West

Leith

Trinity House Museum

National Gallery of Scotland

Nelson Monument

North Berwick Law

Bank of Scotland HQ

Assembly Hall of the Church of Scotland

St Giles Cathedral

The Hub

Arthur's Seat

Caledonian Hotel

St Cuthbert's Church

St John's Church

West Register House

1 The Forth Bridge, completed in 1890, lies eight miles (13km) west-north-west of the castle and is visible on a clear day.

2 The Scott Monument, completed in 1844, lies half a mile north-east of the castle. It celebrates the legacy of the Edinburgh-born writer Sir Walter Scott, who took a keen interest in the castle and was instrumental in the rediscovery of the Honours of Scotland (crown jewels) here in 1818.

4 THE ONE O'CLOCK GUN

'The third day the gun boomed out at one o'clock exactly, frightening the citizens and scattering the flocks of pigeons roosting on the city's buildings.'

Account of the first firing (after two failed attempts), 7 June 1861.

The One o'Clock Gun is fired from Mills Mount Battery at precisely 1pm every day, except for Sundays, Good Friday and Christmas Day. This Edinburgh tradition is witnessed by visitors to the castle and heard for miles around.

A little before 1pm, crowds gather and the district gunner appears in a distinctive dark blue uniform with red-striped trousers. He or she consults a watch, and at exactly the right moment, fires the gun. Its report is heard throughout the city and well out over the Firth of Forth.

This is significant, because the gun was originally introduced as an aid to shipping. In order to navigate accurately, a ship's crew needs to know the exact time, calibrating it with the position of the Sun. In 1861, when the One o'Clock Gun was introduced, clocks were not as accurate as they are today.

2

1

1 One of the blank shells fired in the One o'Clock Gun.

2 The One o'Clock Gun and its gunners in 1861. At that time, the gun was fired from the Half-Moon Battery.

3 As the clock on Mills Mount Battery approaches one o'clock, the gunner prepares to fire.

The gun complements a visual signal: the Time-Ball, introduced in 1853. This is a large sphere at the top of Nelson's Monument on Calton Hill, a mile east of the castle. At 1pm, the ball can be seen dropping a short distance … or it can if the weather is clear. But Edinburgh is often cloudy, so the gun was added. Originally, the two were linked by an electric cable.

The first One o'Clock Gun was an 18-pounder field cannon, of a type now visible around the castle's battlements. Various other types of gun were used until 2001, when the present 105mm field gun was introduced.

 Stand by Mons Meg to get a good view of the Gun being fired. Make sure your watch is accurate and try to catch the flame coming out of the barrel!

Delayed reaction
Sound travels relatively slowly, at about 340m (1,125ft) per second. The bang of the One o'Clock Gun therefore takes about 10 seconds to reach the local ports of Leith and Newhaven, and longer to reach vessels out at sea. Navigators had to factor this into their calculations.

3

5 THE NATIONAL WAR MUSEUM

The National War Museum (part of the National Museums Scotland) occupies the former south ordnance storehouse, built in the 1750s, and the military hospital, built in 1898.

The National War Museum opened in 1933 as the Scottish Naval and Military Museum, the first of its kind in Britain. Its first home was in the Queen Anne Building, next to the Scottish National War Memorial: both were seen as a fitting tribute to the sacrifice made by Scots men and women during the First World War. One in five Scots who enlisted never came home, the greatest proportion of any of the Home Nations.

The museum's outstanding collection presents the story of Scots at war from the creation of the first standing army in the 1600s to the present. It provides a personal perspective of more than 300 years of warfare, through collections of memorabilia and weapons relating to extraordinary individuals. Some of the displays explore the daily life of Scots servicemen, along with accounts of battles lost and won.

One of the most fascinating stories is the transformation of the Highlanders – once considered rebellious – into the ideal soldiers of the British Empire.

A recent addition to Museum Square is the fine equestrian statue of Field Marshal Earl Haig, gifted to the city in 1923 by Sir Dhunjibhoy Bomanji of Bombay. The statue had stood on the Esplanade for almost 90 years before it was moved to allow installation of new stands for the Royal Edinburgh Military Tattoo. The War Museum contains collections related to the Field Marshal.

1

From the parapet there are excellent views over the New Town towards the Forth Bridges and the Ochil Hills. Best time: late morning.

2

1 The bronze statue of Field Marshal Earl Haig, commander of the British Expeditionary Force during the First World War. It was moved here from the Esplanade in 2011.

2 A regimental drum of the South Fencible Regiment, dating from the late 1700s.

3 'The Thin Red Line', painted by Robert Gibb in 1881, shows the two-man-deep battle formation successfully deployed by the 93rd Highlanders at the Battle of Balaclava in 1854.

3

4 Two of the German airmen shot down near Edinburgh in 1939 and treated in the military hospital in the castle.

5 Eric Kennington's well-loved portrait of Lance Corporal Robertson of the 11th City of Edinburgh Battalion of the Home Guard.

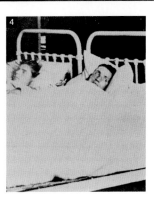

4

5

6 THE GOVERNOR'S HOUSE

The pleasing Georgian residence halfway up Hawk Hill from Mills Mount Battery was built in 1742 for the castle governor. Lodgings for his principal staff officers, the master gunner and storekeeper, were provided in the two wings.

The post of governor was suspended in 1876, and reinstated in 1936 as an honorary title for the General Officer Commanding land forces in Scotland. In the interim, sisters from the castle hospital used the building. Today, it serves as officers' mess and residence for the governor, the General Officer commanding the Army in Scotland. It is not open to visitors.

Each new governor is installed during a splendid ceremony conducted on the Esplanade by the Lord Lyon, King of Arms – the Scottish official responsible for heraldry. During the ceremony the governor also becomes a member of the royal household in Scotland.

7 THE NEW BARRACKS

Behind the Governor's House is the enormous New Barracks, built during the wars with Napoleonic France. The seven-storey building still serves a variety of military purposes.

Work began in 1796, the year Napoleon married Josephine and swept through northern Italy. It was finished in 1799, the year the great general became undisputed leader of his country.

This vast building housed an infantry battalion (600 officers and men). It is not the most handsome structure in the castle. Sir Walter Scott likened it to 'a vulgar cotton mill', and his contemporary, Lord Cockburn, was overheard to say: 'Look on the west side of the castle – and shudder!'

The only part of the New Barracks normally open to visitors is the Regimental Museum of the Royal Scots Dragoon Guards (see page 20).

1 The Governor's House, an elegant Georgian building of 1742.

2 The rainwater hopper is embellished with the inscription GR3, for King George III.

3 The New Barracks, completed in 1799, and still used by the army.

Independent museums devoted to two of Scotland's oldest regiments are housed in the New Barracks and the Drill Hall opposite.

8   The Regimental Museum of the Royal Scots Dragoon Guards

'I saw Ewart, with five or six infantry men about him, slashing right and left ... Ewart had finished two of them, and was in the act of striking a third man who held the Eagle; next moment I saw Ewart cut him down, and he fell dead ... Almost single-handed, Ewart had captured the Imperial Eagle of the 45th "Invincibles".'

An eyewitness account of Waterloo by Scots Greys Corporal Dickson, published in 1911.

The Royal Scots Dragoon Guards was formed in 1971 through the amalgamation of two cavalry regiments – the 3rd Carabiniers and the Royal Scots Greys.

The Scots Greys were raised in 1678 to help Charles II suppress the Covenanters (religious dissenters). Their first battle was at Rullion Green, in the Pentland Hills just south of Edinburgh. Two Regiments of Horse, raised in 1685 and later designated Dragoon Guards, merged in 1922 to become the 3rd Carabiniers.

The museum tells the regiment's history, from the bloody European wars of the 1700s to the global struggles of recent decades.

Pride among the exhibits are the Eagle and Standard of the 45th French infantry, captured at Waterloo in 1815, and the sword of their captor, Sergeant Charles Ewart. A painting of the event now hangs in the Great Hall. Ewart was later promoted to ensign. In 1938, his body was removed from its original grave to a grand tomb on the Esplanade.

1 One of the six Victoria Crosses awarded to soldiers of the Royal Scots during the First World War.

2 'Scotland Forever!' by Lady Elizabeth Butler shows the Royal Scots Greys in action at Waterloo. It can be seen in the National War Museum.

3 The Imperial Eagle of Napoleon's 45th 'Invincibles', captured by Sergeant Ewart at Waterloo.

4 'Foog's Gate' inscribed on the archway that bears that mysterious name.

5 A view of Foog's Gate.

Foog's Gate was built in the later 1600s, during a major refortification of the castle commissioned by King Charles II. The origin of the name is unknown. It was previously known as 'Foggy Gate', referring perhaps to the haar – a thick sea mist that shrouds the Castle Rock from time to time. The walls on both sides of the gate have openings for cannons and muskets.

 There's a good shot of Foog's Gate framing Saint Margaret's Chapel. This looks especially good first thing in the morning with nice shadows.

9 Museum of the Royal Scots and the Royal Regiment of Scotland

The Royal Scots (The Royal Regiment) is the oldest infantry regiment in the British Army. It was raised in 1633 by Royal Warrant of Charles I to serve Louis XIII of France. The regiment finally joined the British Establishment in 1678.

The Museum displays the uniforms, medals and other items of a regiment that first served at Tangier in 1680 and won a further 146 Battle Honours – including all Marlborough's major battles, the Peninsula and Waterloo, campaigns in India and China, the Crimean and Boer Wars, both World Wars and the Gulf War.

In the First World War (1914–18) the regiment expanded to over 100,000 men in 35 battalions, suffering 11,213 killed and over 40,000 wounded. The six Victoria Crosses won during that war are on display.

In 2006, the Royal Scots amalgamated with five other regiments to form the Royal Regiment of Scotland. One room of the museum is now dedicated to this regiment, with displays featuring objects related to recent operations and other aspects of modern military life.

11 ST MARGARET'S CHAPEL

This tiny structure is the oldest building in the castle, indeed in Edinburgh. It was built around 1130 by King David I as a private royal chapel. He dedicated it to his mother, Queen Margaret, later St Margaret.

Margaret was an Anglo-Saxon princess who married Malcolm III. She died at the castle in 1093, just days after learning that her husband and eldest son had been killed in an ambush. Three of her other sons became kings of Scotland: David was the third of them. Reputedly very pious, she was canonised as a saint in 1250.

Try a shot from St Margaret's Chapel at about 3–4pm, looking north-east over the Scott Monument. Good in bright weather, though an overcast sky can be atmospheric.

The chapel was probably part of the first stone-built royal lodging in the castle, housing a hall and private chambers. It may have resembled a Norman tower-keep, of which a few examples still survive in England. The rubble walling on the entrance side had to be infilled when it became a separate building, in contrast to the squared ashlar blocks around the other three sides.

This was the only building left standing in 1314, when King Robert Bruce ordered the castle to be put beyond the use of the English, out of reverence to this royal saint. But the chapel still bears the scars of siege damage, with burnt and reddened stonework on its south side.

Although plain outside, the chapel is a delight inside. A fine chevroned arch divides the small space into two – a semi-circular chancel, housing the altar, and a rectangular nave for the royal family's use. The chapel became redundant in the later 1500s, when royal use of the castle ended. It was later converted into a gunpowder store – the stone-vaulted 'bomb-proof' ceiling dates from then.

The chapel's original function was rediscovered only in 1845, by the antiquarian Sir Daniel Wilson, who then supervised its restoration. The stained-glass windows of St Andrew, St Ninian, St Columba, St Margaret and William Wallace were added in 1922 by Douglas Strachan, who also designed the windows in the Scottish National War Memorial.

The tiny chapel is a wonderful place for a christening or a wedding, and the ladies of the Guild of St Margaret maintain the furnishings in memory of their namesake who died here in the castle over 900 years ago.

1 The exterior of St Margaret's Chapel.

2 Douglas Strachan's stained glass window depicting St Margaret.

3 The chevroned arch dividing the nave from the chancel.

The miracle of Margaret

Inside the chapel is a case containing a copy of St Margaret's Gospel book *(above)*, her favourite devotional work, which she diligently studied.

Although Margaret was later revered as a saint, her biographer recounts only a single miracle during her lifetime, when Queen Margaret was travelling and this precious book fell out of her saddle bag into a river. A servant was sent back and found the gospel, immersed but undamaged. A Latin poem added to the beginning of the gospel-book describes the event. The original manuscript is in the Bodleian Library, Oxford.

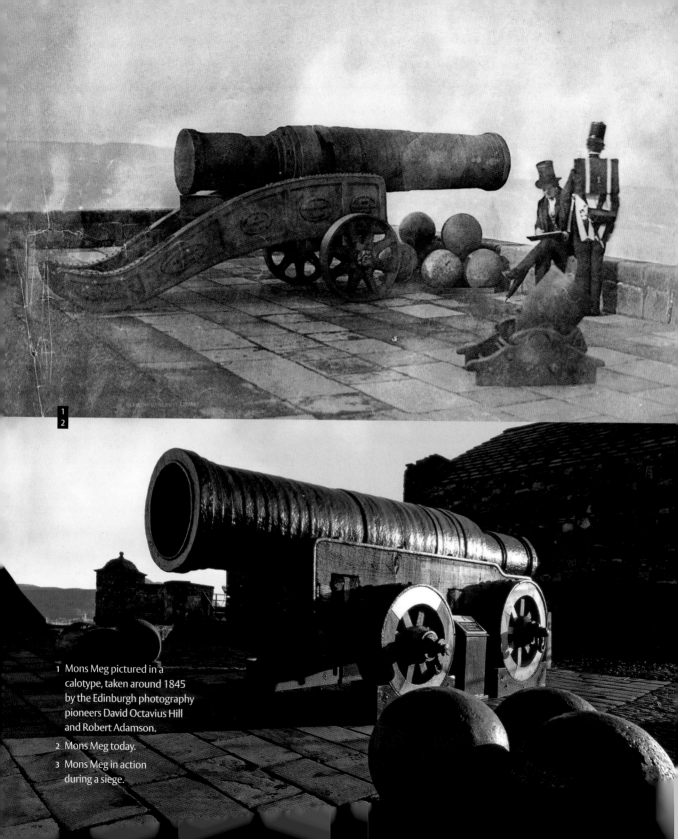

1 2

1 Mons Meg pictured in a
   calotype, taken around 1845
   by the Edinburgh photography
   pioneers David Octavius Hill
   and Robert Adamson.

2 Mons Meg today.

3 Mons Meg in action
   during a siege.

12 MONS MEG

Weighing six tonnes, with a bore of 19in (48cm), Mons Meg is possibly the largest gun ever fired in anger in Britain.

In 1449, when this bombard (siege cannon) was forged in the Belgian town of Mons, she was cutting-edge military technology. She could fire a stone ball almost two miles (3.2km).

The Duke of Burgundy sent Mons Meg as a gift for James II in 1457. The king was family, having married the duke's niece, Mary of Guelders. James was known to be enthusiastic about artillery, but this was an extraordinary present. The arrival of such a powerful weapon underlined the growing confidence and strength of both king and kingdom.

We do not know whether Mons Meg was taken to Roxburgh Castle when James besieged it in August 1460. She was not easy to transport, and could only cover nine miles (15km) a day. In the event, another cannon exploded close to the king, who died of his wounds.

In 1489, James II's grandson, James IV, sent Mons Meg and other cannons to attack the rebel-held castles of Duchal, Crookston and Dumbarton in the west of Scotland. They quickly surrendered rather than face the wrath of Mons Meg.

Her next recorded excursion came in 1497, when she was dispatched to Northumberland to besiege Norham Castle. She departed in style, covered with a fine painted cloth and serenaded by a troop of musicians. But the attack was not a success. The English garrison held out and the bombard trundled slowly home.

When James IV mounted his next raid into England – the campaign of 1513 that cost him his life – Mons Meg was no longer needed. Her place had been taken by bronze cannons that could fire more destructive iron balls. As military ordnance, she was obsolete.

But Mons Meg found a new role, firing deafening salutes to mark occasions of national importance. In 1558, she was fired to celebrate the wedding of Mary Queen of Scots. The gunstone was later recovered from Wardie Muir, now within the Royal Botanic Garden.

Although used as a weapon during the Lang Siege (1571–3), Mons Meg continued in her ceremonial role. She even started to attract visitors.

Meg's last salute came in 1681, when she was fired to mark the birthday of the Duke of Albany – later King James VII. A charge of particularly potent gunpowder burst her barrel – you can still see the damage. Mons Meg was then unceremoniously dumped within the castle and lay neglected for many years.

In 1754, Mons Meg was taken to the Tower of London, along with other inoperative guns, in the wake of the Jacobite Risings. But she was not forgotten.

In the 1820s, campaigns were launched to have this icon of Scotland's heritage returned. On 9 March 1829, Mons Meg was given a military escort back to the castle through cheering crowds. The grand old lady had finally come home.

Wait your turn to get a picture. Mons Meg is a popular subject, but a shot of someone next to her helps give an idea of scale.

The British are renowned for their love of dogs, and this little cemetery is proof. Since the 1840s it has served as a burial place for regimental mascots and soldiers' pet dogs.

Here lie faithful hounds such as Jess, band pet of the 42nd Royal Highlanders (the Black Watch), who died in 1881, and Dobbler, who for nine years until his death in 1893 had accompanied the Argyll and Sutherland Highlanders to such exotic locations as China, Sri Lanka and South Africa.

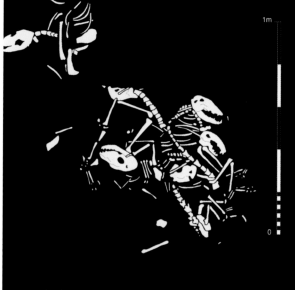

Unearthed

In 1988, archaeologists digging just outside the service entrance to the vaults under Crown Square made a grisly discovery. They found a pit filled with the skeletons of at least 25 dogs. They had all been killed at the same time and buried here in the early to mid-1600s. This had been an industrial area at the back of the Gunhouse, well away from the elite quarters on the other side of Crown Square.

This was a mixed bunch of 25 small to medium-sized dogs, ranging from terrier to small collie types. Some were old and infirm pets, while most probably formed a mixed hunting pack, maybe even belonging to the royal household. Their skeletons were mainly intact and so we know they had not been butchered for food. Once buried, the pit had been sealed with clay, suggesting that all the dogs in the castle had been rounded up and slaughtered, probably because of fears of disease. This was a common occurrence, and for example we know that there was a mass slaughter of cats, dogs and pigs in Edinburgh at a time of plague in May 1585.

Artefacts found with the dogs led the archaeologists to believe that this cull had possibly happened around 1640, when the castle was besieged by Covenanter forces.

1 A gravestone in the dog cemetery.

2 The Argyle Tower seen from above.

14 THE ARGYLE TOWER

The Argyle Tower is in effect the upper part of the Portcullis Gate, added to that older structure in 1887.

It was designed by Hippolyte Blanc, an Edinburgh architect, as part of the same scheme as the restoration of the Great Hall. These works were all financed by the Edinburgh publisher, William Nelson. Blanc and Nelson wished to add grandeur by heightening the tower in the imagined style of the later 1300s.

The tower houses an exhibition about Victorian schemes to 'improve' the castle (see also pages 28–9).

Nelson had hoped the tower might become the permanent home of the Honours of Scotland, the Crown Jewels, but he died disappointed.

The tower is named after the 9th Earl of Argyll. He is said to have been imprisoned above the Portcullis Gate on the night before his execution on 30 June 1685, for leading a failed rebellion against James VII. Argyll reportedly dined well and slept soundly the night before his execution, and went to his death defiant to the end.

Looking at Edinburgh Castle today, it is hard to imagine the many stages of its development. After centuries of change, some dramatic alterations took place during the reign of Queen Victoria (1837–1901).

Walter Scott's rediscovery of the Honours in 1818 boosted the castle's popularity as a visitor attraction. In the decades that followed, Britain's fascination with all things medieval grew.

By 1850, it was widely felt that the castle was not impressive enough: an active military fortress, rather than the medieval stronghold and royal palace of old. Schemes were launched to render it more 'castle-like'.

In 1853 the architect and antiquarian Robert Billings proposed a new church on the site of the North Barracks, where the Scottish National War Memorial now stands. Colonel Richard Moody presented plans for an armoury in the form of a medieval keep. Queen Victoria and Prince Albert, planning their own fairytale castle at Balmoral, indicated approval, but nothing came of either scheme.

Attention then turned to the New Barracks. Francis Dollman aspired to recast it in the Scots Baronial style, but his plans were rejected. He found more favour in 1859, with a fanciful vision for a French-style château. Work began, but the project was halted.

After Albert's death in 1861, the architect David Bryce proposed a new baronial keep as a monument to him. This plan only failed because Victoria wished her husband's memorial 'to stand by itself, unconnected to any other work'.

However, some plans were realised, and form part of the castle fabric today. These include the Argyle Tower and the interior of the Great Hall. The architect and driving force behind these was Hippolyte Blanc.

Despite his French name, Blanc was born and raised in Edinburgh. He joined His Majesty's Office of Works in 1865, becoming its Chief Assistant in 1877. Blanc was recommended by William Nelson, a publisher and public benefactor. Nelson had stepped forward in 1883 to finance the restoration of the Great Hall, then serving as a hospital, and the building of the Argyle Tower. He hoped the tower would become a permanent home for the Honours of Scotland.

Blanc began work, but in September 1887 Nelson died. Almost immediately, Blanc fell out with the army over his failure to keep them informed of progress. In early 1888 the army complained that a new doorway had been inserted without approval. Restoration work was halted for most of that year.

Further conflict arose when the army wanted to use the Great Hall as an armoury. Blanc declared he had restored it as a medieval hall, and refused to hand over the keys on completion in November 1891. The formal opening in October 1892 was a muted affair.

Meanwhile, the military architect R. Lawson Scott was working on a new gatehouse. This replaced a much simpler gate of the 1600s, and was intended to make the castle look more like an imposing medieval fortress. The new entrance opened in 1888.

With the Great Hall remodelled, the army was left without a hospital at the castle. The ordnance storehouses behind the Governor's House were converted and a new military hospital built in 1897. These buildings now house the National War Museum.

1 David Bryce's proposal for a baronial keep as a memorial to Prince Albert.

2 The castle's main entrance as it looked before the Gatehouse was added in 1888.

3 The Edinburgh architect Hippolyte Blanc.

4 Francis Dollman's re-imagining of the castle in the style of a French château.

The Victorian additions to the castle still excite argument. The Gatehouse is one of its most iconic structures, but it masks much older features. Similarly, the Great Hall's interior may look Victorian, rather than evoking the medieval grandeur Hippolyte Blanc had in mind.

Whatever opinions prevail, the personalities and politics that influenced the buildings still fire the imagination with thoughts of what might have been.

15 THE FOREWALL BATTERY

The Forewall Battery was built in the 1540s, approximately on the line of the medieval defences. It was substantially reconstructed after the Lang Siege of 1571–3. It is now armed with cast-iron guns made during the wars with Napoleonic France.

The Fore Well

At the bottom of the deep, rock-cut shaft of the Fore Well is one of the most treasured commodities in Edinburgh Castle – water. For centuries, it was a lifeline for the garrison.

But when the well was pumped dry towards the end of 1913, the Fore Well was revealed as a time capsule for the castle's often violent history. William Thomas Oldrieve, the 59-year-old principal architect for Scotland, was lowered 33.5m (110ft) to the bottom in a bucket. He found the upper 7m (23ft) were made of circular courses of neatly cut blocks before the shaft suddenly opened through igneous vaults to a roughly hewn square shaft.

The upper section was built when the Half-Moon Battery was constructed in the 1570s. But the lower part is much older, dug out more than 700 years ago. It was first recorded in 1314, shortly after the castle was recaptured from the English. At that time the well was filled in to make it impossible for future invaders to hold the site. It was cleaned out again in 1381 and continued to provide the castle with water for almost 200 years until siege damage choked off the supply once more.

Water was always in short supply in the castle. In 1573, the garrison was forced to surrender when the Fore Well was jammed with debris during the Lang Siege. In another siege in 1689, the castle's defenders had to surrender after drinking the well dry. Oldrieve calculated that the well held 130,000 litres – simply not enough to resist a long siege.

At its bottom was further evidence of war. Fragments of explosive shells and a cannonball were found, as well as a sponge used to clean inside a cannon, four hammer heads, two coins and a brass uniform button.

16 THE HALF-MOON BATTERY

The impressive curved wall of the Half-Moon Battery gives Edinburgh Castle an appearance unrivalled anywhere else in the world. It was built after the Lang Siege, over and around the ruin of David's Tower, to serve as the castle's chief high-level defence on its vulnerable east front.

Following the 1689 siege it was repaired much as you see it now. Until 1716, the battery was armed with the famous 'Seven Sisters', bronze guns cast in the castle for James IV around 1500. The battery was also the first home of the One o'Clock Gun.

A good place to photograph cannons. Try shooting through a gun embrasure and 'blasting away' at the Scott Monument. The gilding on the Palace also looks great in the morning with crisp shadows.

1 Soldiers of the 92nd Gordon Highlanders on the Forewall Battery, in a photograph of April 1846 by David Octavius Hill and Robert Adamson.

2 A helmet of the later 1500s, found in this part of the castle. It may have been worn by one of the defenders during the Lang Siege of 1571–3.

3 A set of gun gauges, used to measure cannonballs.

4 The Half-Moon Battery viewed from the east.

17 DAVID'S TOWER

Within the Half-Moon Battery lie the ruins of the once-mighty David's Tower. This was the heart of the castle in the late 1300s, named after King David II, who had it built.

Originally standing over 30m (100ft) high and bristling with arrow slits, this colossal structure took nine years to build, and wasn't complete when David died in 1371. Part of the basement and principal floors survive, and these atmospheric ruins can be accessed by a stair at the back of the Half-Moon Battery.

This was the royal residence at Edinburgh Castle for almost 100 years, where successive kings could welcome foreign diplomats and intimidate their nobility in grand surroundings.

That grandeur is long gone, but we can still imagine the two-storey-high hall, where visitors entered the king's presence, with painted walls and an embroidered canopy over the throne.

David II had spent years in England and France, living in fine stone towers. On his return he was intent on creating his own statement in stone as a reflection of his power and kingship. His tower thrust out from the curtain wall, looking down on everyone who approached the castle – friend or foe.

1

It was tremendously strongly built, with thick walls which stepped in as they went higher. It accommodated the royal household in comfort, with a chamber for the king and another for the queen, stacked in floors above the hall. At its top were battlements and a fighting platform; at its foot was one of the main entrances to the castle, protected by a strong barbican – a covered entrance passage.

By 1433, James I had added another tower just behind David's Tower. This contained the 'great chamber', a much larger feasting space. A passageway connecting the two towers still survives.

By the early 1500s, David's Tower had been eclipsed as a royal residence by the Royal Palace, which had developed from the great chamber. But in troubled times, David's Tower was still an important defensive structure. Its walls were thickened by about 2.5 metres on the town-facing side, better to withstand cannon fire. Blockhouses were also added to either side of the frontage. Guns sat atop these, and records survive of a cannon mounted on the top of David's Tower.

The end of David's Tower came dramatically, during the civil war that followed the abdication of Mary Queen of Scots. On 22 May 1573 it was reported that 'a great part of David's Tower fell', choking the Fore Well and bringing an end to the two-year Lang Siege.

Soon afterwards, the Half-Moon Battery was built around the shattered stump of the tower, which then lay hidden for more than 300 years. It was only rediscovered in 1912.

The ruins of David's Tower are partly obscured by later cellars, built after 1573 as siege barracks. They were bomb-proof, but couldn't keep out disease. It was probably here that many of those killed during the 1689 siege died, most likely of water poisoning.

1 A cutaway illustration shows how the interior of David's Tower may have looked.

Death on the menu

The legend of the Black Dinner recalls one of the most shameful episodes in the castle's history: the assassination of the 16-year-old William, 6th Earl of Douglas, and his younger brother. There are no contemporary records to describe exactly what happened in 1440. But it ended with the boys' deaths.

The chronicler David Lindsay of Pitscottie wrote a detailed, dramatic account a century later, in the mid-1500s. This probably owes a lot to oral traditions and family yarns. But it makes for a tremendous, dark chapter in the castle's story.

The Douglases were the most powerful nobles in the kingdom, who had won favour under Robert the Bruce. By the 1400s, they had rich estates and mighty castles.

Pitscottie records that Douglas boys were invited to the castle to dine with the 10-year-old King James II. They were getting on well when a servant 'presented ane bullis head befoir the earle Douglas, quhilk [which] was ane signe and tokin of condemnatory to the dead'.

At this signal, armed men seized the boys. Pitscottie notes that the young king 'grat verie sore' (wept bitterly) and begged Sir William Crichton, keeper of the castle, to release the Douglases. His tears were in vain: they were dragged to Castle Hill and beheaded.

If the Black Dinner did happen, it would probably have been in the grand first-floor hall of David's Tower. Pitscottie clearly held Crichton responsible for the crime. But it was the boys' great-uncle James Douglas, Earl of Avondale – known as James the Gross – who benefited from their deaths. He inherited the earldom of Douglas, and gained further estates by marrying his son to the boys' sister.

Bad blood between James II and the Douglases did not end here. He personally killed William, the 8th Earl, at Stirling Castle in 1452; and in 1455 he ruthlessly besieged all their major strongholds, finally overthrowing this powerful family.

CROWN SQUARE

Crown Square was created in the later 1400s as the principal courtyard of the castle. It was originally known as the Palace Yard.

Around the four sides of the square were ranged the most important castle buildings:

- the **Royal Palace**, where the sovereign resided
- the **Great Hall**, the major place of ceremony
- the **Royal Gunhouse**, where Mons Meg and the other great guns were displayed
- St Mary's, the Chapel Royal.

The last two have long been demolished and replaced – the Gunhouse by the Queen Anne Building, and St Mary's by the Scottish National War Memorial. Yet Crown Square still retains its ancient atmosphere of enclosed privilege.

By the time Crown Square was formed, the inhospitable summit of the Castle Rock had been gradually shaped, over at least 1,500 years, for the needs of secure living. This top level formed the enclosed 'citadel' – the safest place and thus the preserve of prehistoric chiefs and then medieval kings. Its south-eastern flank was the safest of all, protected by a sheer rock face, so it's not surprising that this side evolved as the royal heart of the castle.

A palace complex began to be created here in the later 1400s, when what had been ancillary buildings at the back of David's Tower took on a greater significance. It was James III who started to plan a more formal arrangement of the chief royal buildings around a grand open space, influenced by ideas from European courts.

The Palace is best photographed later in the day as the sun moves to the west. See if you can grab the narrow view between the Scottish National War Memorial and Queen Anne Building.

Before this, the cliff fell away to the south on the site now occupied by the Great Hall. James III began the difficult but inspired process of building up and out from the southern crags, adding two levels of vaults. This created a platform on which the Great Hall could be built, enlarging Crown Square.

It was James IV who completed his father's work. He built the Great Hall, and regularised the arrangement of the buildings around the Palace Yard, like an Italian Renaissance piazza. At last, the Stewart dynasty had a focal point for its glorious kingship, as well as for the pageantry and spectacle of court life.

The name 'Crown Square' came into use after Sir Walter Scott's discovery of the Scottish Crown and the other royal regalia in the Royal Palace in 1818. During the long period of military use in the 1600s and 1700s, it had been known as the Grand Parade.

A stone plaque in the corner of the square, between the Royal Palace and the Great Hall, records the death here on 11 June 1560 of Mary of Guise. She was the widow of James V, the mother of Mary Queen of Scots and the regent of Scotland from 1554 until she was deposed in 1560. This was a time of great national tension that resulted in the Protestant Reformation.

Temporary resting place

So grave was the political situation in 1560 that Queen Mary of Guise's body had to remain in the castle for nine months before permission was given for it to be taken to France for burial. Her bones now lie in Rheims, but her ghost is still said to haunt the Royal Palace!

Below. A plaque at the south-east corner of Crown Square commemorates Mary of Guise.

MARY OF LORRAINE, QUEEN OF JAMES V. MOTHER OF MARY QUEEN OF SCOTS AND REGENT OF SCOTLAND FROM 1554-1560 DIED HERE 11TH JUNE 1560 "A LADY OF HONOURABLE CONDITIONS, OF SINGULAR JUDGMENT, FULL OF HUMANITY, A GREAT LOVER OF JUSTICE, HELPFUL TO THE POOR"

1 Crown Square in 1829, from an engraving by Thomas Shepherd.

2 Crown Square today. The Royal Palace has changed little, though the Great Hall (right) was restored in 1887–91.

3 A rainwater hopper on the Palace carries the royal cipher of James IV.

This castle was a principal royal residence from the 11th century until the early 17th century. As well as comfortable living quarters, it provided an impressive statement of majesty and might, a repository for royal treasures and registers, and a place of safety in times of strife.

The Palace was the heart of the royal castle. Begun as an extension to David's Tower, it probably contains elements of three separate towers of the 1400s. These include the Register House, which stood between the Palace and the Great Hall.

The straight stair leading down from the Crown Room may have originated as the main access to one of these towers. Little survives of James I's 'great chamber' built in 1434–5 – just the stone-vaulted cellars underneath. But survivals from the later 1400s include two fine fireplaces on the ground floor, in the Laich Hall and its ante-room.

The most important event at the Palace was the birth of the future King James VI, on 19 June 1566. His mother, Mary Queen of Scots, had abandoned the comfort of Holyroodhouse for the birth. The castle was safer, and remained an important symbol of royal power.

1 The Scottish royal coat of arms: part of the wall decoration added to Queen Mary's Birthchamber when her son, King James VI and I, returned to his birthplace in 1617.

2 The legend IR for 'Iacobus Rex' (King James): part of the same decorative scheme.

3 The Laich Hall of the Royal Palace, when transformed into a presence chamber for James VI.

Mary took up residence in the ground-floor chamber, where her furniture and furnishings were installed, including her great four-poster bed. When her time came she withdrew to the tiny room now known as the Birthchamber. It was a long and painful labour.

The delivery of a healthy male heir prompted great celebrations. Above the doorway leading from Crown Square is a gilded panel bearing the date 1566 and the initials MAH, for James's parents Mary and Henry, Lord Darnley. But within 14 months, Darnley had been murdered, Mary deposed, and the infant James crowned king.

In 1603, James became king of England as well as Scotland, and he soon abandoned Edinburgh for London. The castle – particularly the Palace – lost much of its royal resonance.

James returned only once, in 1617, to celebrate his Golden Jubilee – 50 years as King of Scots. His visit prompted major remodelling of the Palace. Exterior features from this time include carvings dated 1615 and 1616, the battlemented parapet and the square turrets with their ogee-shaped roofs.

There are also ornate window pediments carved with royal emblems – the Crown, the Scottish thistle, the English rose, the French fleur-de-lis, the Irish harp and the monogram IR6 (Iacobus Rex 6: 'King James VI').

Two large panels on the east façade displayed the Honours of Scotland and the royal arms of Scotland; the latter panel was defaced during Cromwell's occupation in the 1650s.

Internally, new state rooms were created, including the Laich (low) Hall, lit by large new windows. There were also new apartments for the king and queen on the first floor, now occupied by the Honours exhibition. The Birthchamber was redecorated for James's visit as a shrine to his kingship. On the first floor, a strongroom called the Crown Room was built to house the Honours of Scotland, where they have been secured ever since.

In 1818 the Honours were rediscovered in the Crown Room, where they had been locked away following the Act of Union in 1707. By then, the Palace had spent nearly two centuries in military use. At last it could regain something of its regal glory.

19 THE HONOURS OF SCOTLAND

'The extreme solemnity of opening sealed doors of oak and iron, and finally breaking open a chest which had been shut since 7th March 1707, about a hundred and eleven years, gave a sort of interest to our researches, which I can hardly express to you, and it would be very difficult to describe the intense eagerness with which we watched the rising of the lid of the chest.'

Sir Walter Scott, in a letter to John Wilson Croker, 7 February 1818.

'That the Crown, Sceptre, and Sword of State continue to be kept as they are within that part of the United Kingdom now called Scotland; and that they shall so remain in all times coming, notwithstanding the Union.'

Article XXIV, the Treaty of Union between Scotland and England, 1707.

The Honours of Scotland – the Crown, Sceptre and Sword of State – are the oldest crown jewels in the British Isles.

They were created in Scotland and Italy during the reigns of James IV and James V, and first used together for the coronation of Mary Queen of Scots in September 1543.

The Honours have had an eventful history. Between 1651 and 1660 they lay buried to preserve them from the clutches of Oliver Cromwell, first at Dunnottar Castle, near Stonehaven, and then under the floor of nearby Kinneff Church. After the 1707 Treaty of Union they were locked away in the Crown Room and forgotten.

Then in 1818 Walter Scott, with royal approval, had the room broken into. The oak chest in which they had been kept was forced open. He found them lying exactly as they had been left 111 years earlier.

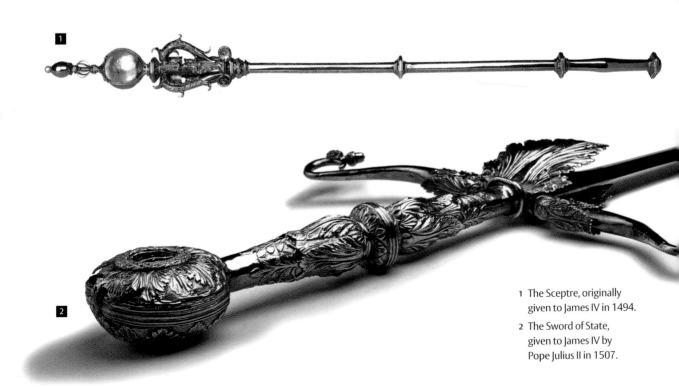

1 The Sceptre, originally given to James IV in 1494.

2 The Sword of State, given to James IV by Pope Julius II in 1507.

The Crown was made for James V in 1540 by John Mosman, an Edinburgh goldsmith. Mosman melted down the gold from the old crown, added more Scottish gold to it, and studded the new circlet with gemstones. The king first wore his new crown at the coronation of Queen Mary of Guise in Holyrood Abbey in 1540.

The Sceptre was presented to James IV, probably in 1494 by Pope Alexander VI. James V had it lengthened in 1536 by the Edinburgh silversmith, Andrew Leys. The upper part of the rod, decorated with Scottish thistles, is Leys's work.

The Sword of State, with its scabbard and belt, was presented to James IV by Pope Julius II in 1507. All three items were created by the Italian cutler Domenico da Sutri. The fracture in the sword's blade and the crease in the scabbard were probably made before The Honours were smuggled out of Dunnottar in 1652.

3 The Crown, made in Edinburgh and first used in 1540.

4 The padlock from the chest in which the Honours were found in 1818.

5 The elaborate orb and cross on the top of the Crown.

Since the Honours of Scotland were placed on display, they have been joined by other pieces of royal and state jewellery.

The silver-gilt wand was discovered in 1818, nestling alongside the Honours in their oak chest. A metre long, it is topped with a crystal globe and a gold cross. Its origins and function are unclear. Walter Scott suggested it might be associated with the Lord High Treasurer, whose mace is described in a document of 1616.

The Stewart Jewels were taken to France by James VII when he fled into exile in 1688. The ruby ring is said to have been worn by his father Charles I at his English coronation in 1626. The other pieces are personal insignia, associating the king with chivalric orders: the St Andrew Jewel of the Order of the Thistle, and the Collar and Great George of the Order of the Garter.

James bequeathed these pieces to his son, Prince James Francis Edward (the Old Pretender), who in turn left them to his own son, Prince Charles Edward (Bonnie Prince Charlie). When Prince Charles died in 1788, they passed to his younger brother, Prince Henry, Cardinal York.

Henry had become a Catholic cardinal in 1747, the year after his brother's defeat at the Battle of Culloden. He was a powerful figure in Rome until Napoleon's invasion of 1796.

He fled to Venice, where he lived in poverty, but refrained from selling the Stewart Jewels. Ultimately he received financial assistance from King George III, a symbolic end to the longstanding rivalry between their families.

Henry died in 1807, and left the Stewart Jewels to George III, whose son, George IV, had them returned to Scotland in 1830.

The Lorne Jewels are later additions, bequeathed to the people of Scotland by Princess Louise, daughter of Queen Victoria, in 1939. They comprise a necklace, locket and pendant made from pearls, emeralds, sapphires and well over 300 diamonds. These priceless items had been given to her by Clan Campbell when she married John Campbell, Marquess of Lorne, in 1871.

3

4

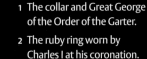

1

2

1 The collar and Great George of the Order of the Garter.

2 The ruby ring worn by Charles I at his coronation.

3 The Lorne Jewels, given to Princess Louise by the Campbells of Lorne.

4 The silver-gilt wand, found with the Honours in their oak chest.

THE STONE OF DESTINY

On 30 November 1996, Edinburgh Castle became home to another Scottish treasure – the Stone of Destiny. Don't be fooled by first appearances; this battered stone was an icon of the medieval Scottish nation, vital to the kingmaking process.

For centuries, early kings of the Picts and Scots were inaugurated at the ancient royal centre at Scone, near Perth. The Stone (also known as the Stone of Scone) is a large block of local sandstone, traditionally believed to have been part of a royal bench-throne imbued with sacred powers. Each new king was ceremonially lifted onto the throne by leading nobles. A great royal monastery was established at Scone around 1120. This reinforced Scone's role as an enthronement place, and its importance continued into later medieval times.

Edward I of England began the Wars of Independence in 1296, asserting his God-given (as he believed) right of superiority over Scotland. To help achieve this he forcibly removed the Scots' royal regalia and holy relics, along with 65 chests containing the records of the kingdom – in short, the objects of statehood. He made sure that the kingmaking Stone was included in his haul. It was removed from the abbey of Scone in August 1296.

Edward sent the Stone to Westminster Abbey in London, where he had it enclosed within a new gilded throne, the Coronation Chair. The Stone has been used ever since in the coronation ceremonies of most monarchs of England, and, from 1714, all the rulers of Great Britain.

But of course another Scot was enthroned on the Stone. James VI and I was made king of England at Westminster Abbey in 1603, fulfilling the prophecy that Scots would reign wherever the stone lay.

The Stone was returned on the 700th anniversary of its removal, and now rests again in Scotland. It will only ever leave Edinburgh Castle when there is a coronation in Westminster Abbey.

1 The Stone of Destiny.

2 The stone crossing the River Tweed into Scotland during its historic journey in 1996.

Two dates with destiny
On Christmas Day 1950 four Scottish students removed the Stone of Destiny from Westminster Abbey. On 11 April 1951 it turned up 500 miles away – at the high altar of Arbroath Abbey!

The Great Hall was completed in 1512, to serve as the chief place of royal ceremony in the castle. It was built for James IV, who was killed at Flodden barely a year later.

The medieval hammerbeam roof is one of the most important in Britain. Scientific analysis has shown that the oak timbers were felled in Norway around 1510, and then shipped to Edinburgh. The stone corbels supporting the main trusses are carved with Renaissance symbols, the oldest surviving in Britain, including symbols of James's kingship and his amity with England and France.

In the little time he had to enjoy his new banqueting chamber, James made the most of it. In June 1513, he hosted a splendid feast to mark the signing of an alliance with the young Irish chieftain Manus O'Donnell, with music provided by the chieftain's own harper (see page 63).

A spectacular space but with low light levels, and usually other visitors. Try detailed shots of the armour, weapons and stained glass. Set your camera to wide angle and get close in.

The walls have ears
The iron-barred opening to the right of the great fireplace was a peephole (called a 'laird's lug' in Scotland), from where the king could spy or eavesdrop on his courtiers. The KGB asked that it be bricked up prior to Mikhael Gorbachev's state visit in 1984.

1 The interior of the Great Hall, as restored in the 1880s.

2 The oak hammerbeam roof, crowning glory of the Great Hall, completed in 1512.

Arms and armour
Displayed in the Great Hall is a spectacular collection of military arms and armour, on loan from the Royal Armouries. This includes spears, bill-hooks, halberds, two-handed swords, basket-hilted claymore swords, Lochaber axes, pistols, armour and helmets for pikemen, cuirassier cavalry armour, mortars of the 1600s, cavalry swords and naval boarding axes and pikes.

James's son and successor, James V, preferred the more comfortable Palace of Holyroodhouse, but the Great Hall was still used. Banquets were held here, with the king and honoured guests at the high table by the great fireplace, and other guests seated at tables groaning with delicacies and fine French wines. Nobles gathered here before processing to Holyrood or the Tolbooth for Parliaments and other meetings of state.

On 2 September 1561, Mary Queen of Scots, newly returned from France, slipped into Edinburgh Castle through the postern gate with her court and nobles. They sat down to a splendid dinner at noon, before beginning a procession from the castle down the Royal Mile to her home at Holyrood, accompanied by a booming salute from the castle guns.

When Cromwell captured the castle in 1650 he had this large space converted into soldiers' barracks, and it remained in military use for the next 230 years. Cromwell's troops created a large central doorway, now blocked but still visible from outside. The hall was fitted out with three floors of galleries, wide enough to hold rows of beds.

This makeshift arrangement lasted until 1737, when the hall was fully converted into sleeping quarters, on three floors with fireplaces in the end walls. New windows were created to light the separate floors.

The Great Hall served as the main barracks until the New Barracks opened its doors in 1799. It was then converted into a military hospital, with its hammerbeam timbers masked by a whitewashed ceiling.

In 1886, work began to restore it to its former glory (see page 28). The architect Hippolyte Blanc orchestrated almost everything inside – the impressive hooded fireplace, the heavy Gothic timber entrance screen and panelling, the heraldic stained glass, the lighting and flooring; all except the great medieval timber roof.

21 THE SCOTTISH NATIONAL WAR MEMORIAL

The souls of the righteous are in the hand of God.
There shall no evil happen to them.
They are in peace.

The words around the walls of the Shrine, taken from
the Apocrypha 3, 1–3.

The Scottish National War Memorial was created in
the 1920s to honour the dead of the First World War.
In later years, it was used to commemorate those who
fell in the Second World War and later conflicts.

In medieval times, the north side of Crown Square
was occupied by the castle church of St Mary. David II
reconstructed this as his Chapel Royal in 1366, possibly
influenced by the erection of the splendid chapel at
Windsor Castle, which he had seen during his long
years of captivity in England.

1

Following James V's development of Holyrood Palace,
the church was converted into a munitions store in 1538
for the fast-expanding royal arsenal. It was eventually
demolished in 1754 and replaced by the North Barracks,
which could accommodate 270 men on three floors.

When the garrison left the castle in 1923, the opportunity
was taken to adapt the barracks as a memorial to the
dead of the First World War (1914–18). The architect was
Sir Robert Lorimer, and the cream of Scottish artists and
craftspeople were employed in its creation. The Prince
of Wales (the future Edward VIII) formally opened
Scotland's National Shrine on 14 July 1927, with the
elderly Field Marshal Haig by his side. The building now
also commemorates the fallen of later conflicts.

The exterior of the building is enriched with sculpture
symbolising the 'Just War'. The animals in the windows
and niches represent the Vices and Virtues; the figures on
the Crown Square elevation signify Courage (mailed figure
with sword and shield), Peace (a female figure with doves),
Justice (blindfolded with scales and a sword), and Mercy
(a warrior cradling a child). Above the entrance, the figure
rising from a phoenix illustrates the survival of the spirit.

Inside is the Hall of Honour. Here the enormous
contribution of Scotland's 12 regiments and the other
corps and services are recorded. Beyond lies the Shrine,
focused on the steel casket containing the complete
Roll of Honour of the Scottish dead. The figure of
St Michael the Archangel soars overhead, and the
stained-glass windows and bronze friezes give vivid
impressions of the First World War.

1 A stained glass roundel shows buglers playing
the 'Last Post', a call associated with military funerals.
2 The south wall of the Hall of Honour.

NEUVE CHAPELLE · LOOS · SOMME · ALBERT · GUILLEMONT · BEA

2

THE QUEEN ANNE BUILDING

The Queen Anne Building was constructed as military accommodation, following a Jacobite Rising in 1708. It now contains tea rooms, a function suite and education facilities.

The building was designed as quarters for officers and gunners. It has two storeys, with rooms arranged around a long central courtyard.

We know from archaeological investigations that a large medieval building previously stood in this location. It was built in the late 1300s during the major reconstruction of the castle. It had a single storey at the level of Crown Square, supported on two floors of basements behind.

Unearthed
Excavations have revealed that the top floor of the Royal Gunhouse was completely destroyed in the Lang Siege of 1571–3. The deep basements survived, and a new narrow range of buildings was constructed here in the early 1600s, associated with a new gun battery and defensive wall just to the west, all supported by the vaults below.

This became the Royal Gunhouse, where the artillery was kept, and was home to Mons Meg from her arrival in 1457. Artillery workshops were outside and in the basement, keeping the sounds and smells of industry away from the royal court.

The south basements of this range were altered in the early 1500s to create a kitchen for the new Great Hall, capable of catering on a mammoth scale. Huge supplies of food and drink were delivered via a newly constructed west entrance. A small army of kitchen hands rushed the meals up a steep stair to the Great Hall.

In the 1750s, the vaults beneath the Queen Anne Building and Great Hall found an entirely new use – as accommodation for prisoners of war (see page 48).

1 The two sides of a board-game piece, made from antler, found during excavations under the building. It dates from the 1400s, when the Royal Gunhouse stood here.

2 The Queen Anne Building, added to Crown Square in 1708.

23 DURY'S BATTERY

This gun battery, defending the castle's south side, is named after Captain Theodore Dury. He was the military engineer who designed it – as well as the Queen Anne Building – after the 1708 Jacobite Rising.

When the vaults beneath Crown Square were used to house prisoners of war, this confined space was used as an exercise yard. The inmates spent much of their days here, and were able to trade with the Edinburgh townsfolk via the perimeter fence. They made a meagre income selling objects crafted from walrus ivory, old soup bones, bits of wood and bedstraw. Scale models of ships and intricate little workboxes were the most popular purchases. The more resourceful prisoners forged banknotes!

24 THE MILITARY PRISON

The Military Prison was built in 1842 for offending soldiers from the garrison, who were locked up for offences such as 'drunk on guard'.

In the 1880s it was extended, increasing the number of cells from 12 to 16, and providing separate ablution blocks, and rooms for the provost marshal, the officer in charge.

The prison was a miniature version of the great civilian prisons of the day. The prisoners were held in solitary confinement, and compelled to do four hours of hard punishment a day – such as carrying cannonballs from one place to another.

3 Dury's Battery in use as an exercise yard, when the vaults below Crown Square housed prisoners of war.

4 The Military Prison, where offending soldiers were disciplined from 1842.

Scuppered!

Twenty pirates from the Caribbean were imprisoned in the vaults in 1720. They had been captured off the west coast of Scotland with a ship's hold full of gold. They were brought to the castle pending their trial. Most were found guilty of piracy and hanged below the High Water Mark off Leith.

PRISONS OF WAR

Beneath the Great Hall and Queen Anne Building are two tiers of cavernous stone vaults, entered from Dury's Battery. Over the centuries they were used as stores for food and military supplies, soldiers' barracks, kitchens and bakery, state and military prisons. But their use as a prison of war captures our imagination most.

The first prisoners of war were the French crew of a privateer captured in the North Sea. They arrived in 1758, soon after the outbreak of the Seven Years' War with France. By the end of the war in 1763 they had been joined by 500 more.

The vaults were also used in this way during the American War of Independence (1775–83). Once again almost all the prisoners were sailors, but this time they included not just Frenchmen, but Spanish, Dutch, Irish – and of course Americans.

Some of those 'damned Yankees' were in fact Scots who had emigrated to North America and become caught up in that momentous event. They included two sailors from the fleet of Captain John Paul Jones, 'father of the American Navy', who was himself a Scot.

The wars with Revolutionary and Napoleonic France (1793–1815) saw the climax of the vaults' use as a prison of war. Again most of the inmates were sailors, including a five-year-old drummer boy taken at Trafalgar (1805), but soldiers later arrived from Portugal and Spain, where Lieutenant General Sir Arthur Wellesley (later the Duke of Wellington) won some important victories over Napoleon's forces. The prisoners came from many different backgrounds, and in the crowded, squalid conditions, feuds developed between the various nationalities.

Escape was never far from their minds. One prisoner hid in a dung cart but died on the rocks below when the contents were tipped over the castle wall.

Four more escaped in 1799 by lowering themselves down the rock on washing lines. The most audacious breakout occurred in 1811, when 49 prisoners cut their way through the parapet wall beside the battery; all but one escaped. The hole is still there.

1 Inside one of the recreated dormitories where prisoners of war slept.

2 One of the iron grille doors that helped contain the prisoners.

3 Graffiti carved by one of the inmates during the American War of Independence.

4 A bone piece ingeniously carved by one of the prisoners to forge Scottish banknotes.

LEAVING THE CASTLE

As you make your way out of the castle, you will pass through a series of gateways belonging to different periods in its history.

The Portcullis Gate

This fortification dates from the 1570s. As you leave, notice the decorations just outside its archway. The stone panel above the outer gate is decorated with hearts and stars, the armorial insignia of James Douglas, Earl of Morton. He commissioned the Portcullis Gate when he was Regent of Scotland for the young James VI.

The shield displaying the Lion Rampant, the Scottish Royal Arms, was inserted in 1887, when the decorative upper story, the Argyle Tower, was added.

A plaque high up on the south wall records the exploits of Sir William Kirkcaldy of Grange, who commanded the castle during the Lang Siege.

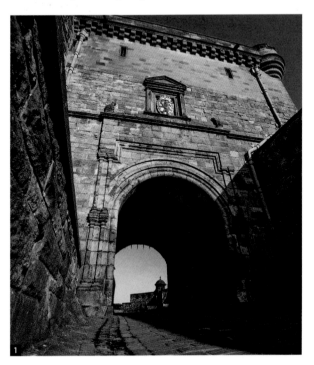

The Inner Barrier

The next gateway you will pass through is the Inner Barrier, dating from the 1600s. Now reduced to a pair of stone gateposts and a sturdy, sloping wall, it was originally much more formidable, defended by a pit and a 'flying bridge', operated by counterbalancing weights.

The Old Guardhouse on your left, now a gift shop, began as a gun platform protecting that barrier. When the latter became redundant around 1850, the platform was roofed over and converted into a guardhouse and prison.

The Gatehouse

The Gatehouse was built in 1888 with the sole intention of making the castle look more imposing. It replaced a much simpler gate of the 1600s. Inside the archway, high up on the side walls, are two stone panels depicting Mons Meg and other munitions then kept in the castle. Carved in the late 1500s, these originally adorned the Gunhouse.

Outside, set into the façade, are bronze statues of King Robert the Bruce on the left and Sir William Wallace on the right. These were added in 1929, to mark the 600th anniversary of Bruce's death.

Try a shot of the Royal Mile spires framed by the Gatehouse arch. Head to Princes Street Gardens or Castle Terrace and wait until the golden hour for spectacular shots of the castle.

3

The Esplanade

The Esplanade was formed in 1753 as a parade ground for the castle garrison, and has been used for military spectacles ever since. Each August since 1950 it has hosted performances of the world-famous Royal Edinburgh Military Tattoo.

Prior to 1753, this was a rugged open landscape where the citizens came to watch far more grisly spectacles. Castle Hill was a place of execution, where women accused of witchcraft, religious dissenters and others who had fallen foul of the sovereign were hanged or burned at the stake.

1 The Portcullis Gate, commissioned by Regent Morton soon after the Lang Siege of 1571–3.

2 One of the stone panels depicting Mons Meg and other armaments of the castle. Probably dating from the 1500s, they were incorporated into the much later Gatehouse.

3 Statues of King Robert the Bruce (left) and Sir William Wallace (right), added to the Gatehouse in 1929.

Unearthed

In 1989, archaeologists discovered 15 skeletons below the area where the new ticket facility now stands. The bones belonged to soldiers who had died defending the castle during the first Jacobite Rising of 1689. Their bodies could not be taken for burial in the town because the castle was under siege.

THE HISTORY OF EDINBURGH CASTLE

The volcanic rock at the heart of Edinburgh forms a natural defence, with steep cliffs on three sides. It is not surprising that it has been occupied and fortified for so long.

Habitation can be traced back at least 3,000 years to the Bronze Age. In the early centuries AD an Iron Age fort stood here.

Edinburgh was a royal centre by 1093 at the latest, and throughout the medieval era it was an important royal fortress. Edinburgh was Scotland's capital city by the time of David II (1329–71), and James III (1460–88) took the castle as his main residence, embracing Renaissance ideas from Europe. His son James IV helped bring these to fruition, in the magnificent Great Hall and Royal Palace.

James V developed Holyroodhouse as a more comfortable royal residence and the castle's royal use dwindled, especially after his grandson James VI – born in the castle – became James I of England. However, it still houses the most priceless artefacts of state: the Honours of Scotland and the Stone of Destiny.

Always a place of military strength, the castle was central to the Wars of Independence (1296–1356), the Rough Wooing of the 1540s, the Marian Wars of the 1570s and the Covenanting Wars of the 1600s. It later became an army garrison. It was occupied by Oliver Cromwell's troops, and played an important part in Hanoverian efforts to suppress the Jacobites. Its military role continues, alongside its growing importance as a visitor attraction.

Throughout its long history, Edinburgh Castle has consistently stood as a crucial focus for Scotland's struggles and aspirations, and as a symbol of nationhood.

Right. A painting of 1780 by the Edinburgh-born artist Alexander Nasmyth shows the castle from a position now occupied by Princes Street Gardens. The water at the right is the Nor' Loch, which by then had been partially drained.

EARLIEST TIMES

Edinburgh Castle is a truly ancient fortress. The great rock on which it sits is reputedly Britain's oldest continuously occupied fortified place. A dramatic pinnacle of basalt rearing high over its low-lying surroundings, this was a place of safety, power and wonder.

There were certainly people living here in the Bronze Age. Traces of the hearths over which they cooked their food were found close to the Redcoat Café (see page 9). Most likely they were part of a sprawling, hill-top settlement that radiocarbon dating places between 972 and 830 BC.

2

1

By the first centuries AD, a fort on the Castle Rock housed an Iron Age chief, secure from intruders. Two large ditches near the Gatehouse were hacked out of the rock to defend the settlement at a time when such fortified sites were common across this part of Scotland. But the people who lived in a large roundhouse on the Castle Rock – found in excavations – faced a particularly formidable enemy: the Roman army.

The Romans invaded Scotland on a least three occasions. Their fearsome legions reached as far north as Aberdeenshire. They built forts near Edinburgh, and later a huge supply depot at Cramond, four miles north-west. But neither base was occupied for long.

During this time, the people who lived on the Castle Rock thrived. They definitely had contact with the Romans, proven by the discovery of a wealth of Roman artefacts including brooches and pottery.

c. AD 100

Residents of the hill fort on the Castle Rock trade with the Romans for exotic objects.

c. 640

The local **Gododdin tribe** is conquered by Anglian invaders from the south. Little evidence of their existence survives, aside from this decorated bone comb.

But there are no signs of conquest. Some scholars believe the local tribe, known as the Votadini, were friendly with the Romans. They may even have been allies.

The hill fort on the Castle Rock was clearly an important place. The kings of the Gododdin, as the Votadini became known, may have lived here in the centuries after the Romans departed. It was even celebrated in some of Britain's oldest surviving poetry.

The Gododdin is a collection of verses celebrating their heroes and their allies. In about AD 600, they rode to what is today North Yorkshire to fight the Angles. Much of the poetry describes the warband enjoying a year of feasting in a great hall at Din Eidyn before setting off to battle – the earliest record of Edinburgh Castle. Through the richly descriptive verse, supposedly composed by the bard Aneirin, there is a remarkable but fleeting glimpse of a lost kingdom centred on the Castle Rock.

The warriors were confident of victory:

Never was there such a host
From the fort of Eidyn
That would scatter abroad the mounted ravagers.

But the warband never returned to Edinburgh, slaughtered almost to a man. A few decades later, in about AD 640, King Oswald of Bernicia led a band of Angles north into what is now Scotland. They conquered the Gododdin and the stronghold on the Castle Rock fell. The old name Din Eidyn was anglicised to Edinburgh.

From these tumultuous centuries only a handful of artefacts have been found by archaeologists – a decorated bone comb, some spearheads and other pieces of metalwork. The Angles controlled south-east Scotland for 300 years, until they were driven from the Castle Rock in about AD 960.

1   The Iron Age hill fort as it may have looked around AD 100.

2   A carved stone lioness found at the site of a Roman fort in Cramond, on the outskirts of Edinburgh. The lioness is shown devouring a bound human figure, and probably represents the power of the Roman Empire over the local people.

3   An artist's impression of the Goddodin war party that, according to legend, left Edinburgh around AD 600 to meet the Angles in battle.

CASTLE OF THE MAIDENS

The lands north of the River Tweed – now the Lothians and Borders – were Saxon territory for several hundred years. They were fought over until 1018, when Malcolm II of Scotland defeated the English, as they were now called, at Carham, 50 miles (80km) south of Edinburgh.

In 1093 we read of a royal castle on the rock, known as the 'Castle of Maidens'. Why 'Maidens' is unclear, though there was a story that the Picts used to keep virgins here.

1

In November 1093 Queen Margaret fell gravely ill at the castle while her husband, Malcolm Canmore (Malcolm III), was away fighting the English in Northumberland. Then Malcolm was killed near Alnwick, along with his eldest son. On hearing the news, Margaret succumbed to her infirmities and died, three days after her husband.

In the reign of Malcolm and Margaret's youngest son, David I, Edinburgh Castle became a major royal fortress. This early castle was mainly confined to the rock's summit, and would have been built largely of timber. Only St Margaret's Chapel, on the highest point of the rock, was built of stone.

But it seems likely that the chapel originally did not stand alone, and was in fact an integral part of a Norman-style stone keep, about 17m (56ft) square, which occupied the whole platform to the north. King David knew these new-style keeps well, including one at Bamburgh which was the same size. He may also have built one at Carlisle Castle in north-west England, which had been under his control.

Some of the other buildings and defences were probably rebuilt in stone in the 1200s. But the stone walls did not prove strong enough to withstand the armed might of the English in 1296.

1093

Queen Margaret dies at the castle, a few days after learning of the death of her husband, King Malcolm III.

1174

King William I is captured by the English, who take Edinburgh Castle, holding it until 1186.

X. Malcolme 3 surnamed Canmoir
began his rawne, 1057
He maried Margaret dochter to
Edward ye outlaw sone of Edward
yronsyd kmy of England and wer
buryed at dunfermlyn

Malcolme 3 . Margaret Queine

2

1 Margaret's body was removed secretly from Edinburgh Castle and taken for burial at the abbey she had founded in Dunfermline, Fife.

2 A page from the Seton Armorial, produced in 1591, shows King Malcolm III with his wife Queen Margaret, later St Margaret. She died at Edinburgh Castle in 1093, a few days after learning of her husband's death in battle.

Unearthed
In 1989, archaeologists digging outside the Redcoat Café discovered an ancient cobbled track leading west out of the castle. This may just have been the route along which Queen Margaret's coffin was taken when her body was smuggled out of the castle in November 1093.

ROYAL EDINBURGH CASTLE

Medieval royal households were not based in any one place. The Scottish monarch and his or her entourage flitted between royal residences at Edinburgh, Falkland, Stirling and Linlithgow. They also stayed at grand monasteries, or in the homes of important nobles around the kingdom. The household was huge, consuming vast quantities of food and resources, and so had to move around to allow residences and hosts to restock.

A royal castle had to fulfil certain key functions. It was a symbolic and real centre of power: it provided comfortable accommodation for the king and queen, their household and court; a place of worship; a repository for national records; a secure storehouse for food rents, tax monies and for the royal jewels and regalia; a state prison; and separate accommodation for royal officers. Edinburgh took on these roles to become pre-eminent among Scotland's royal castles.

Kings in the 1100s and 1200s stayed here more than in any other place. But it was not popular with everyone. When **Alexander III** (1249–86) married Margaret, daughter of King Henry III of England, she wrote home, describing her less-than-palatial home on the Castle Rock as a 'sad and solitary place, unwholesome and without greenery'.

David II (1329–71) spent time in exile in both France and England, and became familiar with the finest European architecture of the time. On his return, he set about rebuilding the castle, and had David's Tower raised as his primary residence. The ruined tower is the oldest royal lodging in Scotland.

James I (1406–37) invested in new buildings to improve the castle's royal accommodation. He also had a number of new towers built or repaired. His son **James II** (1437–60) loved big guns, and spent much time close to the royal arsenal, which was kept secure in the castle.

1 James I (1406–37).

2 James II (1437–60).

3 James III (1460–88).

4 James IV (1488–1513).

5 James V (1513–42).

6 The Birthchamber in the Royal Palace, where Mary Queen of Scots gave birth to James, the future king of both Scotland and England.

7 The royal coat of arms of Scotland.

The castle also became the principal residence of James III (1460–88), who may have begun some of the building work that transformed the royal chambers into a Renaissance palace. This grand vision, as well as the magnificent Great Hall, were completed by his son, the illustrious James IV (1488–1513).

James V (1513–42) was brought to the castle for safety as a child king, but later began investing in the royal palace beside Holyrood Abbey, at the foot of the Royal Mile. As well as greater comfort, Holyrood benefited from an excellent water supply, always a problem up at the castle.

From that time, the castle was only used as a royal residence in exceptional circumstances. It remained a great stronghold, continuing to provide protection for the royal regalia, the arsenal, and the archives of the nation.

In 1603, following the Union of the Crowns, the court relocated to London. James VI – now also James I of England – returned in 1617, but he never slept at the castle. The last monarch to stay here was his son Charles I (1625–49) before his Scottish coronation in 1633.

Royal focus returned in 1822 with the triumphant visit of George IV (1820–30), which saw a reconciliation between the Scots and the Hanoverian monarchy. Queen Victoria visited several times between 1842 and 1886, prompting various 'improvements'.

In June 1953, HRH The Queen and the Duke of Edinburgh took part in the Ceremony of the Keys on the Esplanade. She has continued to visit throughout her long reign, and in July 2014 attended the official unveiling of the First World War Memorial Benches.

THE WARS OF INDEPENDENCE

Throughout the 1200s, relations with England had been generally good. But Scotland's succession crisis of the 1290s brought the peace to an end.

Alexander III died suddenly in 1286 and his granddaughter Margaret in 1290, leaving the throne empty, with no clear heir. This led to the 'Great Cause', in which various noblemen launched rival claims to the crown. Edward I of England was invited to adjudicate: he chose a well-qualified candidate, John Balliol, Lord of Galloway. King John was crowned in November 1292.

But Edward now asserted overlordship in Scotland, which ultimately led to a rebellion among John's lords. This, coupled with warming relations between Scotland and France – England's greatest enemy – convinced Edward to launch a brutal war of conquest.

English forces captured Edinburgh Castle in June 1296. They held it for the next 18 years, as a key stronghold in Edward's attempt to subjugate the Scots. Edward pillaged the symbols of nationhood, removing the national archives, the crown jewels and the Stone of Destiny to London.

The castle was eventually won back on 14 March 1314 by Sir Thomas Randolph, Earl of Moray, nephew of King Robert the Bruce. On a dark night, in foul weather, Moray assembled about 30 men below the rock. They were guided by William Francis, who knew of a secret route up the north face of the crag.

1296

King Edward I of England
captures Edinburgh Castle during his first invasion of Scotland.

1314

King Robert the Bruce
captures the castle back from the English and destroys its defences to prevent its reuse.

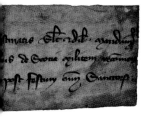

The raiders scaled the castle wall and caught the enemy off guard. This was a great morale boost for the Scots, who overcame a mighty English army at Bannockburn three months later.

The castle was destroyed on Bruce's orders, so it could not be reoccupied by the English. St Margaret's Chapel was the only structure left standing. The castle lay in ruins for 20 years, but on Bruce's death in 1329, war broke out again and by 1335 it was back in English hands. They had to rebuild it from scratch.

The castle was recaptured in April 1341 by Sir William Douglas, in another feat of bravery and cunning. A ship carrying provisions for the English garrison docked at Leith, with 200 Scots masquerading as sailors and merchants. When they arrived at the castle with their consignment, the garrison eagerly lowered the drawbridge. The Scots dropped their wares, jamming the portcullis open, and overcame the guards. Douglas's main force swiftly overwhelmed the English garrison – more than 100 men.

By this time, Edward III of England was embroiled in war with France. This, coupled with increasing Scottish military success, made him abandon his campaign. In June 1341, Bruce's 17-year-old son David II returned from exile to begin his own reign. He made Edinburgh his capital and rebuilt the castle, with David's Tower as his residence and a number of towers providing high-status suites for family and royal officers. A new phase in the castle's life had begun.

1 An artist's impression of the raid of March 1314, by which the castle was won back from the English, three months before the Battle of Bannockburn.

2 A letter of 1300 from King Philip IV of France to his agents at the Vatican, seeking papal support for Sir William Wallace in his struggle to eject the English from Scotland.

3 King John Balliol of Scotland kneels before King Edward I of England. Edward's claim over Scotland led to 60 years of savage warfare.

1335

King Edward III of England recaptures the castle as part of a renewed attempt to subdue Scotland.

1341

Sir William Douglas takes the English occupiers by surprise and reclaims the castle for the Scots.

ROYALTY AND RENAISSANCE

During the 1400s, Europe entered a period known as the Renaissance, a great flourishing of new ideas in the arts, architecture, philosophy and fashion. Its influence was soon embraced by Scottish monarchs, who were keen to position themselves as rulers of a vibrant and prosperous nation.

This desire was partly expressed in costly building schemes at Scotland's royal residences, such as the Royal Palace on the east side of Crown Square. This grand edifice began as an extension to David's Tower in the 1430s, and was further enlarged to become the royal residence itself.

There is little left of the original building, the King's Great Chamber, built for James I in 1434–5. However, the process was completed by James IV in the early 1500s, with the completion of Crown Square as a quadrangle enclosed on all four sides. Its buildings were of a richness and high quality that could reflect the magnificence of his kingship.

It was probably also James IV who created the heart of the palace block we see today, by linking at least two older towers or ranges. The east half of his piazza reflected his majesty and spirituality, while the gunhouse on the west reinforced his martial prowess.

The richness of James IV's Royal Palace can be glimpsed internally in the two fine fireplaces on the ground floor (now the Laich Hall and ante-room), and externally in the stumps of three superb oriels (projecting windows) on the east wall. These would have given the occupants stunning views over their capital, but were badly damaged in the bombardment of 1573 that ended the Lang Siege.

The Stewart kings of this period made some ambitious diplomatic marriages, which also influenced their building schemes.

1

1 Decorative corbels supporting the hammerbeam roof of the Great Hall. Some have been restored, but others survive from the early 1500s, including: A fleur-de-lis, which features in both royal Scottish and Tudor heraldry; the cypher IR4 for 'Iacobus Rex 4' (King James IV); Venus flanked by Tudor roses; A sun with the initials IHS for 'Jesus'; A putto – a cherubic figure representing love.

Marrying for love was fine, but marrying for political advantage – and above all for money – was even better. James II, James III, James IV and James V all married wealthy foreign princesses, whose dowries topped up the royal treasury. These marriages also helped cement important political alliances.

In 1503, James IV (aged 30) married Margaret Tudor (13), eldest daughter of Henry VII of England. This wedding set the seal on a 'Treaty of Perpetual Peace' between the two nations; while Tudor influence extended the process of internationalisation of the Scottish court, in terms of clothing, manners and architecture.

We can see James's confident knowledge of the Northern Renaissance in the carved corbels of his Great Hall, which include representations of the Scottish thistle and English rose. Elsewhere in the Great Hall, the large windows show the influence of French architecture, while the open hammerbeam roof gives a nod to English royal architecture. Similar detailing may well have existed in the Royal Palace, but has since been lost.

Although we know little of the palace James IV created for his young wife, we can be sure that there would have been paired apartments for the king and queen, comprising richly decorated chambers. (Similar arrangements can be seen at Linlithgow and Stirling.) James had adopted new European ideas regarding protecting access to the king, which would have been reflected in the planning of the palace. The higher the status of the visitor, the further they would have been allowed into the suite.

James IV's glorious vision for his palace at Edinburgh was never fully realised. Only ten years after his marriage to Margaret Tudor, he died in battle at Flodden, fighting the army of her brother Henry VIII.

2 James IV and his wife Margaret Tudor, daughter of Henry VII of England. Their marriage was intended to cement a treaty between the two countries.

3 James IV hosts a banquet in the Great Hall in June 1513, a year or so after its completion, and a few months before his untimely death at Flodden.

THE LOST TOWERS

From the 1100s until the late 1500s, the Castle Rock was dominated by spectacular tall towers, designed to project royal power and impregnability. Most have disappeared, for one simple reason: big guns became very effective at demolishing medieval walls.

St Margaret's Tower – A Norman-style keep probably stood at the heart of the castle from the early 1100s, incorporating St Margaret's Chapel. This would have been a fortified residential tower, built from stone, which served as the royal lodgings into the 1200s.

Over time, other stone towers were added around the defensive walls, providing self-contained residences for principal royal officers. Should the castle be attacked, these towers also acted as components of a defensive system. Defenders could shower besiegers with arrows and missiles from protected slits and wall-heads.

The Well House Tower – In the later 1300s, wholesale rebuilding was required as a result of Bruce's scorched-earth policy. This allowed his son, David II, an opportunity to build grand new towers. The Well House Tower was completed by 1366. Sited on lower ground at the north-west side, it protected an important water supply. It also defended the near-vertical route exploited by Moray's assault party in 1314.

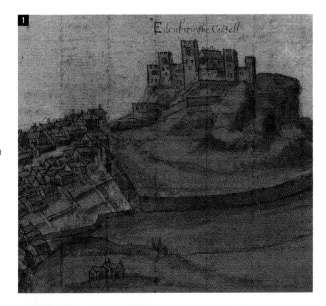

1 A drawing of Edinburgh in 1560 shows the castle with at least five towers. The tallest, at the centre, is David's Tower.

2 A doorway into David's Tower as it survives today.

1544

King Henry VIII of England sends his forces to ravage Edinburgh as part of the 'Rough Wooing', an attempt to marry his son Edward to Mary Queen of Scots.

1561

Mary Queen of Scots holds a banquet in the Great Hall before making a grand entrance into Edinburgh, officially beginning her personal reign.

David's Tower – This was planned as David II's royal lodging. It was the strongest element of the defences, dominating the approach from the town. A sophisticated tower house, it was the prototype of a much-copied form.

Constable's Tower – This tower was built at the north end of the imposing frontage in the 1370s. The constable guarded the castle, and his tower was located by the inner entrance, close to the present Portcullis Gate. Equipped with a drawbridge, it may have been the rebuilding of an older tower. The payments being made for building work at this time suggest other towers were also under construction.

The Great Chamber – This feasting hall was added by James I in 1433. It may have been part of a tower immediately behind David's Tower.

Register Tower – By the 1540s a new purpose-built home for the royal records was needed. This tower was added in 1541–2, between the Palace and the Great Hall. It was an adaptation of an earlier tower of the 1300s.

Other towers are named in the historical record, but now lost, with no clues as to their location. These include the **Jewel Tower** and the **Counting House**, the latter related to the Royal Treasury.

Illustrations made during the 1500s show the castle with multiple towers, but its appearance was radically altered by the Lang Siege of the 1570s.

1566

The future **King James VI** is born in Queen Mary's chambers at Edinburgh Castle. Within 14 months she will be forced to abdicate and he will be king.

The Lang Siege, June 1571–May 1573

Edinburgh's most enduring siege began four years after the forced abdication of Mary Queen of Scots in 1567. She was now being held in England, but the reign of the infant James VI (represented by Protestant lords) was not yet secure. Sir William Kirkcaldy of Grange, an experienced solder, was intent on holding the castle for Mary.

The castle had an impressive frontal defence called the Spur, where many guns were mounted. Its interior was also well provided with guns, with a concentration above the Spur, on top of David's Tower and to either side.

Regent Lennox, grandfather of King James, began the siege. On his death in 1571, he was succeeded by Regent Mar. Neither managed to dislodge Kirkcaldy. Mar died in 1572, and it was his successor Regent Morton who enlisted help from Queen Elizabeth of England.

In April 1573 an English army arrived with guns and mortars. The High Street was sealed off with barriers of earth and turf in an attempt to protect the town. On 21 May the English guns opened up. Before long, David's Tower collapsed onto the Forewall Battery and clogged the well, denying the garrison water. Soon their artillery was destroyed too. On 26 May the besiegers assaulted the Spur with ladders and took it.

Kirkcaldy surrendered on 28 May, and was executed. The castle's capture marked the end of significant support for Mary, and confirmed the success of the Protestant Reformation.

Above. The siege as illustrated in Holinshed's *Chronicles*, published a few years later.

EDINBURGH CASTLE UNDER SIEGE

Welcome to the most besieged place in Britain. We know of at least 26 separate occasions when an attempt was made to take it, by force or by stealth.

The castle had formidable defences, yet surprisingly most sieges were successful. Often, this was because the defenders suffered from disease, shortage of food and munitions, or – crucially – lack of water. As an elevated site, the castle relied on wells for its water supply. When these were exhausted, clogged or maliciously poisoned, the defenders were forced to surrender or die.

From the later 1200s to the later 1600s, the castle garrison was either preparing defences, under attack, or repairing the damage after a devastating siege. This often required total reconstruction of entire buildings, so that only traces of the medieval castle now survive.

The castle's development was shaped by these attacks, and by three episodes in particular. In 1314, King Robert the Bruce ordered its total demolition after it was recaptured from the English. In 1573, the castle was devastated by English artillery, which ended the Lang Siege. And in 1689, Scottish forces wrought extensive damage, endured by Jacobite forces during a three-month bombardment.

To defend Edinburgh Castle

- Ensure you have a minimum garrison of about 200 soldiers, with lots of guns and some skilled gunners.
- Stock up with plenty of supplies and clean water.
- Maintain lines of communication for intelligence and supplies, by slipping past your besiegers at night.
- Put down accurate fire to destroy your attacker's artillery.
- Ignore qualms about collateral damage to people and buildings in the town – even when firing on your own families!

To besiege Edinburgh Castle

- Construct well-protected gun positions and encircling entrenchments.
- Focus on the east front, but ensure complete enclosure all the way around the Castle Rock.
- Ensure that you have a large army of committed troops, with effective guns and gunners familiar with siege tactics.
- Concentrate on the twin aims of destroying your defender's artillery, and wiping out their key buildings and supplies.
- Take your time – starve them out.
- Alternatively, try a sneaky surprise attack, when they are least expecting it. Have a go at undermining the defences, especially from the south side where their guns can't fire down on you.

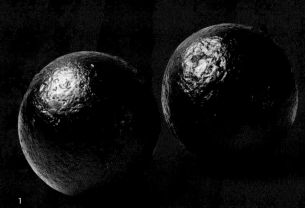

1　A pair of cannonballs found at the castle.

2　David's Tower is destroyed by cannon fire, bringing an end to the Lang Siege of 1571–3.

2

In medieval times, the castle provided real security for the king, who could bask in the reflected glory of its symbolic power and majesty. In times of peace, especially while the royal household was elsewhere, there would only have been a skeleton staff with a small garrison of men-at-arms.

This changed in the 1400s, when the castle took on the vital role of national arsenal. The royal arsenal was maintained here, and new guns were manufactured, ready to deploy when required. The development of increasingly effective artillery went hand-in-hand with the rise of the professional soldier and gunner, well-drilled in new and more scientific siege tactics.

The castle had a reputation for impregnability, but big guns put an end to that.

The importance of guns continued into the 1800s, but the nature of the garrison changed in the 1600s, when the castle ceased to be a royal residence. This new role coincided with the creation of a standing army of professional soldiers, with uniform dress and strict discipline. From then on the castle had to accommodate the chief garrison of Scotland, usually small in number but stuffed with Redcoats at times of crisis.

THE COVENANT AND THE COMMONWEALTH

When Queen Elizabeth I of England died, she was succeeded by James VI of Scotland. This 'Union of the Crowns' was a triumph for the Stewart/Stuart dynasty, but it left Scotland without a resident monarch.

James left Scotland soon after Elizabeth's death in March 1603, and was crowned James I of England on 25 July. He promised to return regularly, but paid only one visit, in 1617, his 50th anniversary as King of Scots. A major remodelling of the Royal Palace was undertaken in preparation for his arrival.

The next king to visit was James's son, Charles I. He returned in 1633 for his Scottish coronation, and was the last reigning monarch to sleep in the castle. Within a few years, Charles's aspiration to reform the Scottish church would lead to conflict.

The turmoil grew from a document drawn up by Protestant dissenters: the National Covenant. Its signatories, known as Covenanters, called on the king to refrain from imposing Catholic-influenced church practices in Scotland. The outcome was armed rebellion, which ultimately drew England and Ireland into the Civil War of 1642–51, and smouldered on in Scotland for decades.

Edinburgh Castle was besieged twice by the Covenanters. In March 1639, their leader, General Alexander Leslie, needed to capture the castle quickly, so he arranged a parley with the Royalist constable. This was a diversion, allowing a bomb to be planted and detonated, blowing off the main gate. Leslie's troops surged into the castle, capturing it in 30 minutes with little bloodshed.

1 The signing of the National Covenant in 1638. This rejection of church reform led to prolonged conflict.

2 Cromwell and his forces at the Battle of Dunbar. A few weeks later they took Edinburgh Castle.

1617

King James VI returns to Edinburgh for his 'Hamecoming' to mark 50 years on the Scottish throne. The castle undergoes major redecoration in his honour.

1633

Charles I visits Edinburgh, and becomes the last reigning monarch to spend the night at the castle.

Fifteen months later, the castle had been restored to Charles I, and its new commander Lord Ettrick was preparing it against attack. The Covenanters again laid siege, billeting troops in houses just below the castle.

A journal written at the time describes an incident when a number of Covenanter officers gathered to dine in one such house. A cannonball fired from the castle smashed through the kitchen wall, and passed through the skirts of the cook. She was not badly hurt, but the disgruntled officers had to cook their own dinner.

Charles I was intent that the castle should hold out. The townsfolk were unsympathetic, and the king ordered Ettrick to fire on them, which he did.

The besiegers undermined the Spur and got into the castle, but the Royalist defenders had foreseen this. The Covenanters were trapped, and most were killed by Royalist fire. The siege turned into a mere blockade, but after three months Ettrick finally surrendered.

Charles I had alienated many Scots, but they were horrified when he was executed in 1649 by Parliament, which then established a republic called the Commonwealth of England. His son, Charles II, was swiftly declared king in Scotland. This provoked an invasion by Oliver Cromwell, a general of the Commonwealth. His troops defeated the Scots at Dunbar in September 1650, then besieged Edinburgh Castle.

Cromwell had limited resources and so attempted an undermining operation from the south. The Scots dropped a barrel bomb, which collapsed the mine. Cromwell then constructed an artillery fort at the top of the Royal Mile, which began firing on the castle.

The Scots' commander, Colonel Walter Dundas, forbade his gunners to return fire, for fear of damaging churches and harming townspeople. Just before Christmas, he capitulated, even though the castle still held supplies to withstand months of siege.

The castle became a barracks for Cromwell's troops, who stripped away its royal finery to establish a military base.

1638

The National Covenant is drawn up in the shadow of the castle. A rejection of Charles I's desire to establish Episcopalian worship in Scotland, it provokes decades of war and strife.

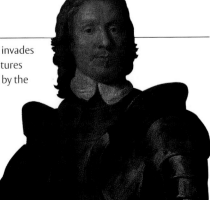

1650

Oliver Cromwell invades Scotland and captures Edinburgh Castle by the end of the year.

CRUEL AND UNUSUAL PUNISHMENT

For all its glamour, Edinburgh Castle once had a reputation as a place of death and torment. People were executed within and outside its walls, and many were tortured in its grim dungeons. Thousands of women and men were accused of witchcraft, and we know that some of them were strangled and then burned on Castle Hill, where the Esplanade stands today.

In 1615, at a time of religious oppression, the Jesuit John Ogilvie was brought to the castle and instructed to name fellow Catholics. He was deprived of sleep for eight days and endured the torture of 'the boot'. This diabolical device comprised four sections of wood bound tightly around the shin; metal wedges were then driven between them to crush the limb. Despite his ghastly ordeal, Ogilvie refused to submit and was taken to Glasgow for a swift trial and a gruesome execution.

In the political turmoil of the 1680s, the 9th Earl of Argyll was implicated in a plot against Charles II. The earl fled, but coded letters in his handwriting were discovered. William Spence, his private secretary, was brought to the castle for interrogation. In July and August 1684, Spence was tortured in a bid to decipher Argyll's code.

Spence was subjected to sleep deprivation and the boot in a dark vault beneath the Great Hall. He was 'pricked' with pins and then faced a new form of torture – the 'thumbikins' or thumb screws, which were introduced from Russia. Spence initially withstood the pain, but his resolve broke when 'he heard they were to put him in boots again [and] being frighted therewith, desired time and he would declare what he knew'.

The 9th Earl was captured the following year and imprisoned in the castle. He spent his last night here – supposedly in a chamber above the Portcullis Gate. He is said to have slept peacefully, and the following day he was beheaded at the Market Cross on the Royal Mile.

1

1 A thumbscrew of the 1600s. This unpleasant torture device was introduced to Scotland from Russia.

Another man implicated in the plot was the Protestant minister William Carstairs. He was brought to the castle and soon cracked under the thumbikins. He was later presented with the instrument used to torment him by the new monarch, William II. The king asked Carstairs to demonstrate the device on him and reportedly roared in pain, declaring that 'under such an infliction a man might confess anything'.

Despite this, King William ordered the torture of the English Jacobite Henry Neville Payne in the castle in 1690. The unfortunately named Payne, who had plotted to restore James VII to the throne, endured the boot and thumbikins but refused to submit.

The Earl of Crawford, who witnessed the torture, wrote of it: 'It was surprising that flesh and blood could, without fainting, endure the heavy penance he was in for two hours.' Payne remained a prisoner in the castle for 10 years. He was Edinburgh's last recorded victim of torture.

The Castle Rock, on which the Esplanade was later built, was for many years a place of public execution. Among the criminals and heretics executed here were as many as 300 people, mostly women, burned at the stake for witchcraft.

The Edinburgh chronicler John Nicoll noted that at least a dozen supposed witches were executed in the 1650s, along with murderers, poisoners, baby killers and men convicted of 'bowgarie and bestiality', one of whom was burned with the cow he was accused of 'lying with'.

One of the earliest allegations of witchcraft came in the trial of Janet Douglas, Lady Glamis. In a politically-motivated case, she was convicted of plotting to poison James V, with evidence acquired through the torture of her family members and servants. In 1537, she was burned at the stake on Castle Hill, a death supposedly witnessed by her son.

Most of those convicted of witchcraft and executed on Castle Hill were not from such wealthy backgrounds. John Fian, a schoolteacher from Prestonpans, was accused of leading a coven of witches to attempt to kill James VI. He refused to confess, despite being brutally tortured – including a stint in the boot – but was convicted regardless, strangled and burned in 1591.

A memorial to those executed on Castle Hill for witchcraft can be seen at the lower end of the Esplanade. Designed by the renowned Victorian artist John Duncan, it is known as the Witches' Well.

2 A European woodcut of 1541 shows the dreaded boot in use.

3 The notorious North Berwick witch trials of 1590–2, during which more than 60 women and men were tortured in Edinburgh and many executed. James VI took a keen personal interest in the case.

THE REDCOAT GARRISON

The decline of Edinburgh's royal role during the 1600s coincided with the emergence of a professional army. Gradually, the castle embraced its new role as a military base.

During Cromwell's occupation, the Great Hall was converted to a barracks, and for many years, the castle held a garrison of around 120 men. But the Jacobite Risings had a major effect on the military presence in Scotland.

In 1688, the Catholic King James VII and II was driven into exile. This was the 'Glorious Revolution', in which Dutch troops invaded to support a Protestant groundswell. The new monarchs were James's Protestant daughter Mary and her Dutch husband William of Orange. They became joint sovereigns on 11 April 1689.

This provoked the first of the Jacobite Risings, all of which attempted to restore the Catholic Stuarts to the throne. In 1689, Edinburgh Castle became the last stronghold in Britain holding out for King James. The Duke of Gordon, a staunch Jacobite, commanded the castle with a force of professional soldiers and 'gentlemen' volunteers.

The besieging forces were led by experienced professionals, and their arsenal included heavy mortars. The garrison was forced to shelter in the castle vaults. Supplies dwindled and many fell ill from drinking dirty water, including Gordon himself.

He eventually surrendered and the Jacobites were released, on condition that they never raised arms against the new monarchs. Every roof in the castle had been destroyed.

After Scotland and England were formally united in 1707, the castle's garrison became part of a much larger army. The term Redcoat was soon widely used, referring to the uniforms worn by soldiers of the British government. The Queen Anne Building was the first purpose-built military accommodation in the castle, intended to house officers and gunners following another Jacobite Rising in 1708.

In 1714, Queen Anne died, ending the Stuart dynasty. She was succeeded by her closest Protestant relation, George I, prince-elector of Hanover. A further Jacobite Rising followed in 1715, when there was a rather shambolic attempt to capture Edinburgh Castle. It failed when the raiders' ladder proved too short for the castle's walls.

1715

Jacobite forces attempting to place *Prince James Francis Edward Stuart* (*right*) on the throne make a doomed attempt at capturing the castle.

1745

Jacobite troops led by *Prince Charles Edward Stuart* (*right*) capture Edinburgh and besiege the castle but lack the firepower to take it.

Rising panic
The folk of Edinburgh have often had a reputation as radicals. When the castle garrison was doubled in 1799, it was partly a response by the Hanoverian government in London to the recent revolution in Paris. It was feared that a similar rebellion might occur in Edinburgh.

1 Jacobites arrested by government troops near Edinburgh in an illustration of the 1740s by Paul Sandby.

2 The Battle of Culloden, 1746: the final defeat of the Jacobite cause.

3 A clay pipe of the 1800s found in the castle.

4 A cartoon of 1819 by George Cruikshank gives vivid expression to British alarm over the French Revolution.

During this period, the castle became a secure lock-up for important prisoners, and a staging post for troops and supplies. The Great Hall barracks was redeveloped in 1737 to expand its capacity to 300 soldiers. In 1742, the Governor's House was built for use by the governor, the storekeeper and the master gunner.

The final Jacobite Rising of 1745–6 was led by Prince Charles Edward Stuart (Bonnie Prince Charlie). His army took Edinburgh on 17 September 1745. He hoped to capture the Honours of Scotland, housed in the castle. These symbols of kingship would have greatly advanced the Stuart cause, but the Jacobites lacked the necessary siege guns. They held the town until marching south on 1 November. Edinburgh Castle was never besieged again.

A new magazine, ordnance stores and cartshed were built between 1749 and 1754. The gun store of the 1500s was replaced by a new barracks for 290 men (now the Scottish National War Memorial). This increased the castle's capacity to 598 men.

In the 1790s, fear of invasion by Napoleon's French forces led to another expansion. The New Barracks was completed in 1799, accommodating a further 600 men, doubling the garrison. However, the end of the Napoleonic Wars in 1815 led to swift demilitarisation. The army was modernised, and the castle entered another phase.

A HISTORY TO CELEBRATE

'The Regalia of Scotland will be opened for the inspection of the public in the Crown Room upon Wednesday the 26th of May instant. 150 persons only will be admitted every lawful day.'

Advertisement in the *Edinburgh Evening Courant*, 24 May 1819

The castle's military functions continued, but over time another role emerged: as a focus for public interest in Scotland's history. This began to grow in the early years of the 1800s.

In February 1818, Sir Walter Scott watched as the Crown Room door was forced open. Inside he found the Honours of Scotland, exactly as they had been left in 1707, following the Treaty of Union with England. They were immediately put on public display.

Among the first to visit them was George IV, during a triumphal visit to Scotland in 1822, partly arranged by Scott. This was the first visit to the castle by a reigning monarch since Charles II in 1651, and an important seal of approval from the Hanoverian monarchy. King George took a shine to tartan, which had been banned during the government's suppression of Jacobite activity in the Highlands.

Another element of this rehabilitation was the mass recruitment of Highlanders into the British Army.

The service of Scottish units in the wars against France, and in winning the Empire, created a heroic image of the kilted soldier, which married well with the re-imagining of Scotland's past. Over time, it came to be expected that the castle would be garrisoned by a kilted Highland regiment, loved by tourists and looking suitably heroic atop the ramparts.

1767

Building begins on **Edinburgh's New Town**. Over time, wealthier citizens will migrate from the crowded Old Town.

1818

The **Honours of Scotland** are rediscovered in their hiding place in the castle.

1 The visit of George IV in 1822 was the cause of great celebration and ceremony.

Dramatic views
Interest in Edinburgh Castle as a historic monument can be traced back as far as Ben Jonson, a younger contemporary of Shakespeare, who enjoyed almost equal success as an actor and playwright in London. He had Scottish ancestry, and in 1619 visited Edinburgh, where he admired the castle and received honorary citizenship. On viewing Mons Meg, he was told that 'one got a woman with child in it'.

Walter Scott's popular historical novels had been an important influence, reigniting public interest in historic buildings. Public pressure now grew to acknowledge the historical significance of the castle and its buildings, and to allow greater public access to them.

In 1829 Scott secured the return of Mons Meg from the Tower of London, where she had been sent after the 1745 Jacobite Rising. The great gun was piped by military bands all the way from the port of Leith to her place on the battlements.

The momentum increased. In 1836, the birthchamber where James VI had been born was vacated by the army and opened to visitors. In 1846 St Margaret's Chapel was recognised among a clutter of buildings. It was restored soon after.

Other more grandiose schemes were projected for the castle. Most never got off the drawing board, but several were completed, including the new Gatehouse at the main entrance in 1888, to make the castle look more like a 'real castle', and the restoration of the Great Hall in 1891 (see page 28).

This new role for the castle, as ancient monument and visitor attraction, was confirmed in 1905 when responsibility was transferred from the War Office to the Office of Works (now Historic Scotland).

1822	1829
George IV visits Edinburgh amid great pomp and ceremony.	**Mons Meg** returns to Scotland and takes pride of place at the castle.

A MODERN MILITARY BASE

In 1815, the 42nd Royal Highlanders marched through cheering crowds lining their route to Edinburgh Castle. Their triumphant return after the Battle of Waterloo brought the city to a halt.

Yet within a year, government austerity measures saw massive army cutbacks. The castle's distinguished military career seemed to be dwindling – but this proved not to be the case.

Throughout the 1800s, many military units were based at the castle before being shipped out around the British Empire.

Monuments around the Esplanade tell of conflicts in India, Afghanistan, Crimea and South Africa. They also indicate the esteem in which these regiments were held.

In 1838, the 78th Highlanders brought an elephant back from Ceylon, now Sri Lanka. The animal led parades through Edinburgh – and reportedly developed a taste for beer. Its toes survive, now displayed at the National War Museum in the castle. It was immortalised on the regiment's insignia and its monument on the Esplanade.

Public interest in heritage was growing, and the castle was invaded by a new army of visitors. Some key buildings were surrendered – the officers' quarters in the Royal Palace, the master gunner's storehouse in St Margaret's Chapel and the military hospital in the Great Hall.

The army also installed state-of-the-art facilities. The military prison was built in 1842, embracing new ideas on discipline. Detention in its centrally-heated, individual cells replaced brutal floggings.

With the restoration of the Great Hall (see pages 28 and 42), a new military hospital was needed. A modern complex was completed in 1897: its buildings now house the National War Museum.

Yet conditions for the garrison were poor. As late as 1906, soldiers in the New Barracks had no proper lavatories, and just six baths between 650 men. In 1909, work began on Redford Barracks in Edinburgh's southern suburbs.

1

1916

John Maclean is handed over to the military authorities at Edinburgh Castle, after campaigning against the war as a socialist and pacifist. He is released to the civil authorities following a public outcry.

1939

A **Luftwaffe bomber** crash-lands near Edinburgh, the first German aircraft to be brought down over Britain in the Second World War. The airmen are treated in the castle's hospital.

However, before Redford was completed, the First World War broke out and the castle returned to active service. It became a recruiting depot, training centre, hospital and prison.

As in earlier conflicts, prisoners of war were held in the vaults. Among them was Karl Burgdorff, who in 1916 scrawled poetry on a wall. The crew of an armed merchant raider added further graffiti. Other prisoners included socialists like John Maclean and David Kirkwood, deemed a threat to civil order.

The castle itself became a target. In April 1916, German Zeppelin airships bombed Edinburgh, killing 13 people. One bomb hit the Castle Rock.

A demobilisation centre was established at the castle to assist Scottish servicemen after the war. The Scottish National War Memorial was opened in 1927, commemorating the thousands who had lost their lives.

The castle served again during the Second World War. In October 1939, four injured German airmen were treated in its hospital after the first air raid of the war. They were visited by the Spitfire pilots who had shot down their bombers.

A cunning effort to mislead German intelligence was launched at the castle during 1944. Operation Fortitude North was a ruse, designed to convince the enemy that an invasion of Norway was imminent, drawing away forces from Normandy, where the D-Day landings would be staged.

Colonel Rory MacLeod co-ordinated the subterfuge, broadcasting phoney military radio traffic, planting bogus newspaper articles (including one about a bagpipe performance at the castle) and feeding information to double agents. The decoy operations room remained until 1958.

1 The cap badge of the 78th Highlanders, with the regimental elephant at its centre.

2 The 78th Highlanders at Edinburgh Castle, in a lively painting of 1861.

3 A recruitment poster of 1933, with Edinburgh Castle in the background.

4 Soldiers of the Black Watch regiment bid their families farewell at the castle before departing for Egypt, in a painting of 1882.

EDINBURGH CASTLE TODAY

Today the ancient royal castle is as much a powerful symbol of Scottish nationhood as it was in centuries gone by.

It is an icon of Scotland's heritage, where two of the nation's greatest treasures, the Honours of Scotland and the Stone of Destiny, are displayed. The global significance of the castle was recognised in 1995 when it became part of the UNESCO World Heritage Site of the Old and New Towns of Edinburgh.

The castle has also become the spiritual home of Scotland's proud military past, through the presence of the Scottish National War Memorial and three military museums. The honorary post of governor is always held by the General Officer Commanding land forces in Scotland, while the Georgian New Barracks still houses an important army command.

Two famous guns reside at the castle: medieval Mons Meg, long since silent, and the One o'Clock Gun, still very much active.

The castle is also home to the world-famous Royal Edinburgh Military Tattoo, staged for three weeks every August, to coincide with the Edinburgh International Festival. The Tattoo began in 1950 as a modest event, with military bands of pipes and drums marching on the Esplanade. Now it is one of the world's greatest spectacles, showcasing the talents of musicians and performers from all over the globe. It has an annual audience of 220,000, seated in impressive temporary stands.

As a visitor attraction, Edinburgh Castle goes from strength to strength. At time of writing in 2014, the castle had broken all previous records with more than 1.4 million visitors in a year – second only to the Tower of London among paid-for visitor attractions in Britain. It had also been named Best UK Heritage Attraction at the British Travel Awards for three years running.

In recent years, the castle has found a new role as a music venue, hosting major concerts during the summer, when the Tattoo seating stands are in place. After thousands of years, this ancient fortress is still adapting to changing times.

1 A military brass band at the castle in 2014.

2 A summer concert on the Esplanade.

1995

Edinburgh Old and New Towns are officially inscribed as a UNESCO World Heritage Site, with Edinburgh Castle as their centrepiece.

1996

The Stone of Destiny returns to Scotland, 700 years after it was taken by Edward I of England.

Open Doors
Since 1993, Edinburgh Castle has been welcoming more than 1 million visitors every year. Not bad for a fortress designed to keep people out!

2

DISCOVER HISTORIC SCOTLAND

There are 25 other Historic Scotland properties in Edinburgh and the Lothians, a selection of which are shown below.

Craigmillar Castle

The substantial residence of Sir Simon Preston, a favourite of Mary Queen of Scots, who was his guest here following her life-threatening illness in 1566.

↗ 3.5 miles SE of Edinburgh city centre

🕐 Open all year. Winter: closed Thu/Fri

📞 0131 661 4445

🚗 Approx 4 miles from Edinburgh Castle

Crichton Castle

Set above a tranquil valley, Crichton was home to numerous colourful characters, including the third husband of Mary Queen of Scots.

↗ 2.5 miles SW of Pathhead, off the A68

🕐 Open summer only

📞 01875 320017

🚗 Approx 15 miles from Edinburgh Castle

Blackness Castle

Built in the 1440s and later repeatedly refortified, Blackness is a daunting and distinctive stronghold over looking the Forth.

↗ 4 miles NE of Linlithgow on the Firth of Forth

🕐 Open all year. Winter: closed Thu/Fri

📞 01506 834807

🚗 Approx 18 miles from Edinburgh Castle

Dirleton Castle

This powerful fortification is among the oldest now surviving in Scotland, and is at its most picturesque in summer when the gardens are in full bloom.

↗ In Dirleton village, 3 miles W of N Berwick

🕐 Open all year

📞 01620 850 330

🚗 Approx 23 miles from Edinburgh Castle

P Car parking
P🚌 Bus parking
🚻 Toilets
♿ Disabled toilet
♿ Reasonable wheelchair access
📺 Interpretive display
🛍 Shop
🍴 Picnic area
☕ Self service tea/coffee
🚍 Accessible by public transport
👟 Strong footwear recommended
🚲 Bike parking
👓 Children's quiz
🕐 May be closed for lunch

For more information, visit:
www.historicenvironment.scot

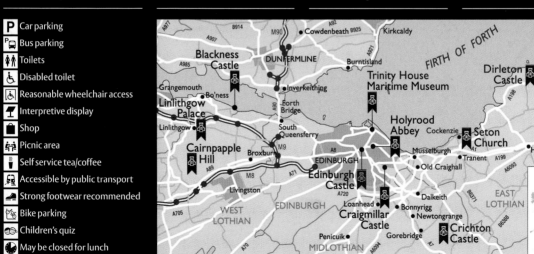